LIVE

A MANIFESTO FOR A CREATIVE LIFE

BIG

ROCHELLE SELTZER

Book design by Mary Lester
marylesterdesign.com

Author photo by Liz Linder
lizlinder.com

Library of Congress Control Number: 2019911990
ISBN 978-0-578-55835-6

LIVE BIG PRESS™

P.O. Box 470802
Brookline, MA 02447
www.LiveBigPress.com

Printed in China
First Printing 2019

LIVE BIG PRESS and DISCOVERY DOZEN are trademarks of Rochelle Seltzer

LIVE

A MANIFESTO FOR A CREATIVE LIFE

BIG

ROCHELLE SELTZER

Life is too precious
to live small.

Foreword

LIVE BIG.

Why?

Because most of us go through life believing we are small, that we don't deserve to live our dreams, or that we aren't good enough.

We spend years pleasing others, hoping to be liked, longing to belong.

We play victim. We feel afraid. We live small.

And yet, deep down inside, in the space where our soul lives, we know that we are more. That we are bigger. That we matter.

And sometimes, a day may come when we wake up and realize we missed out on experiencing all the gifts that life wanted us to have. And that day may be too late.

That's sad. And I don't want that for you.

What I want for you is a life worth living. A life that matters. You know what I mean, right? The kind of life that will bring a smile to your face as you look back, knowing you savored every moment. That you've made a difference. That you truly loved.

Living big is a way of being and a way of doing things. It may not come naturally to you. And that's ok. After all, you are human. You weren't given permission to live big. You may have been born into a family that raised you to see the world through their small eyes.

But guess what? You are more.

You ARE bigger.

And, you have permission.

Permission to grow.

Permission to dream.

Permission to become.

Living big is a mindset. And a practice.

This book is a hands-on manual that can help you step into a bigger space in your life. It can help you connect to parts of yourself that have been waiting for your attention. It's a book of risks, of unfamiliar territory, and of taking chances.

But most of all, this book is a book of action. One step at a time, do the work, and you will begin to live into what your soul has wanted you to experience ever since you got here.

And that's an awesome way to live.

You're in good hands. Rochelle Seltzer has passed through the gates of fear and created a life for herself where living big is the norm. She will gently guide you and tenderly hold the space for you to meet yourself and grow.

Allow this book to lead you to where your heart and soul want you to go.

Peleg Top
Mentor to Creative Souls
Santa Fe, New Mexico 2019

Introduction

THIS IS MY MANIFESTO FOR LIVING BIG.

My path to coaching started when I dared to dive into the mystery of creativity. Although I started my career as a designer, and was often complimented for being "creative," deep down I did not believe I could create in a personal way. The mystery of creating felt completely out of reach for me, but I yearned to understand it.

With loving guidance, I ventured to dive deep into learning, and in tandem I started to access the creativity I had kept hidden most of my life. One step at a time, I dared to start living a fully expressive and authentic life. And I created a new reality for myself.

I now help my clients create their richly rewarding, authentic lives and futures. I guide them to leverage their creative power. I teach them to embrace themselves as creators.

This is what I came to call living big, and it has become my mission to help people everywhere to do that.

While we can each create our own definition for what it means to live big, there are universal and fundamental concepts that I believe are central to a life that is truly big. My definition of living big does not have to do with owning a grand house or acquiring expensive possessions. Rather, I consider attributes like courage, love, passion, creativity, and authenticity to be keys to a beautiful, rich life. It is fundamentals like these, cultivated over time, that are included in this manifesto—a small book about big and important ideas.

We all live a journey. And we all learn as we live and grow.

Some of us find ourselves on a smoother road than others, but nobody gets to travel a direct and easy route all the way through life. Some of us get stuck along the way or make unfortunate turns. Some of us find ourselves traveling a road that was mapped by others and realize it's not our true path, not the one we want to be on. Some of us are able to course-correct easily and move ahead smoothly. Some of us have more difficulties or find our routes more challenging to navigate.

My journey has brought me to places I never foresaw early in my life. I have learned deep and important lessons along the way as I have navigated common potholes and speed bumps, and also some major challenges and significant detours. I now live more fully and more happily than I ever did before, which led to writing this manifesto. Quite simply, I want to share what I have learned.

As you will see, the components of this manifesto are divided into two sections: the *being* and the *doing* of living big. I check in with myself often to see if I am aligned with my definitions of my highest states of being and if I am actively engaged in the actions I have defined as my truth.

Because the concepts in this manifesto have been such a powerful force in my life, I want to help you bring those that speak to you into *your* life, in deep and meaningful ways. You will see that each of the tenets in the manifesto is followed by a short essay and a series of exercises to help you experience each concept. Please use the exercises as a starting point to your exploration. Extend that exploration in as many creative ways as you wish. The exercises are offered to you as a launch pad for you to experiment with and shape your own relationships to the concepts.

It's worth noting the way that I initially connected to each of the concepts in this book. I started my process of identifying and exploring them by completing an important partial sentence that I used to mine my heart. I finished the sentence, *"When I live big, I ..."* with 12 different endings, e.g., *"When I live big, I slow down and am still."* As you will soon see, this powerful exercise, which I call the Discovery Dozen, is fully explained and is included throughout the book. You will have an opportunity to use it in many forms and at many different times as you work in various sections of the book. I hope you will continue to use this tool in your own way in many situations and that you will find it a meaningful way to discover wisdom you already possess, but may not have been able to readily access.

You are on your journey through life and you have the opportunity to create the life you want. I hope that the ideas and exercises in this manifesto will help you as you create your biggest, happiest, most fulfilled life—and live big.

With love,

Rochelle Seltzer
Creative Core Coach

How to use this book

WHILE SOME READERS WILL WANT to start on page one and read sequentially through to the end of this book, I created *Live Big* to be a resource that can be used in many ways. Rather than reading in a linear way, as you would most books, I recommend that you approach the content in any way you need and want on any given day.

You may want to flip through and start reading a subject that intrigues you, or excites you, or that you find to be a challenge in your life.

You may want to start by reading a topic in the *Being* section and stay with others in that section for a while, or you may prefer to skip around the book.

It's fine to start with a topic in the *Doing* section, if you see something there you want to focus on right away.

Or, try randomly choosing topics throughout the book.

If you read through much of the book first, you may then decide to do some of the exercises. Or jump in with exercises as you go. You can certainly skip past any exercises that you're not up for as you choose others to try.

I also recommend that you return periodically to repeat some exercises. You may find that you are at a new starting place a few weeks or months after you originally tried them out.

This book is yours. Embrace it, enjoy it, and use it in the way that has the most meaning for you each time you pick it up.

Meet the Discovery Dozen™ Exercise

WHEN YOU SEE THIS SYMBOL throughout this book, know that my powerful Discovery Dozen exercise follows. Here's how it works:

I'll give you the opening phrase of a fill-in-the-blank sentence. You'll then complete that sentence 12 different ways. Don't overthink it! The idea here is to tap into your intuition and go with whatever comes up for you as you write. Let yourself be playful—even outrageous!

If you feel stuck, just keep writing. Be sure to complete each Discovery Dozen sentence 12 times. This will get easier for you the more you use the Discovery Dozen exercises.

You will also see this symbol on some exercises—what I call the Discovery Dozen Plus. In these cases, I will guide you to choose one or more of the sentences you completed in your first Discovery Dozen exercise, in order to go deeper and discover even more. I will show you how to create a new set of Discovery Dozen sentences based on the first sentence you chose, so that you can expand on or find more information about that key idea.

You will find gems among your answers, each of them mined from your heart.

Get familiar with some important terms

AS YOU MOVE THROUGH *Live Big,* you will find references to several terms that are central concepts to understanding and truly living big. They include:

Self-Love

THE IMPORTANCE OF SELF-LOVE cannot be overstated. When we truly accept, love, and appreciate ourselves; acknowledge our gifts; and feel deserving of all we desire—as well as goodness of every kind in our lives—we are able to be powerfully creative.

The Self-Critic

THE SELF-CRITIC IS THAT VOICE WE HEAR that fills us with doubt. It tries to sabotage us in many ways, such as comparing ourselves to others, procrastinating, feeling like an impostor, perfectionism, and being gripped with fear. Bolstering self-love fortifies us against these tendencies. And building awareness of when and how the self-critic steps in allows us to manage it.

Right Brain and Left Brain

THERE ARE TWO HEMISPHERES IN OUR BRAINS, which are often referred to as the "right brain" and the "left brain." A simple explanation is that the right brain is where ideas are generated. It's the seat of imagination and the source of intuition and inspiration. The left brain is the domain of logic, data, and facts. Both are important! I advocate for appreciation of and focus on the amazing gifts of the right brain because they are vital to being a powerful creator.

THE **BEING** OF LIVING BIG

THE **DOING** OF LIVING BIG

THE BEING OF LIVING BIG

We are human beings, but we spend most of
our time doing, rather than being.
Your state of being is key to living big.

SLOW DOWN AND BE STILL

The magic of quiet
and STILLNESS.

Living big and being quiet at the same time once seemed contradictory to me. But a significant part of living big is my ability to slow down, be still, and be quiet with myself. There is peace and joy in that quiet.

Being constantly "productive" disconnected me from myself. Our culture celebrates speed, productivity, constant accomplishment, and having tech devices connected all the time. I was often too wired to think clearly or get the rest my body desperately needed.

When I am quiet, when I meditate in stillness, when I sit surrounded by the wonder of nature or savor a lovely cup of tea without multitasking, I take care of myself in precious ways. I connect deeply to myself and I live big.

When everyone around us is moving fast, frantically trying to cram more into a day than is possible, when we focus on maximizing productivity in every moment, it's seductive to think this is "normal."

It's easy to push ourselves to live and work that way without pausing to consider that this pace takes a huge toll. The cumulative impact of the physical and mental exhaustion, the anxiety, the stress, the impatience, and the short-temperedness we experience is enormous. And, more than that, the distance we create from ourselves is astounding.

If you never hit the pause button, you never reflect. You don't breathe deeply and consciously. You don't consider your options. Instead, you're constantly reacting and then simply moving on to the next thing.

You may feel trapped—and, in many ways, you are when you live this way. It's time to get out of the high-speed lane, to practice taking pauses, to do a little "nothing" now and then, to benefit from the opportunities to reflect, think, savor, make considered choices, and create the life you want.

1 Sit for 10 minutes and do nothing.

YOU CAN DO THIS ANYWHERE. You can make a date with yourself to do nothing. Try and find a good spot to people-watch; or look for a beautiful place in nature and simply sit and take in the vista; or sit in a museum and contemplate the art in a gallery. See which ways and places feel the calmest and most relaxing for you, or enjoy the variety of being in different places to do nothing.

After you have done this exercise three times a week for two weeks, sit longer at each of these special breaks. Work your way up to 10 minutes of doing nothing each time.

2 Complete this sentence 12 times.

THIS DISCOVERY DOZEN is a great way to tap into both the emotions you're holding and a range of ideas you can generate related to bringing stillness into your life.

"If I sit quietly, I _____."

For example, your completions could include, *"If I sit quietly, I will feel anxious."* Or, *"If I sit quietly, I might get a new idea."* When you have written 12 different endings, see if you feel surprised or inspired by some of your answers. Repeat the exercise at least twice this week and compare the sentences on each list.

③ Spend 5 minutes simply breathing.

THIS CAN BE DONE AT YOUR DESK, after you've parked your car, just before you go to sleep, or any time at all. Start by doing this exercise every other day. After you set a timer for five minutes (so you won't be distracted and check how much time has elapsed), start the exercise.

To get the most benefit, take in a breath and focus on the feeling of the cool air entering your nostrils. Then become aware of the feeling of the air moving through your throat and deeply into your lungs. Pause a moment as the breath you took circulates in your body. Then exhale very slowly. Feel your diaphragm contract, and feel the exhalation rise through your throat. Finally, notice the sensation of how the air exits your nostrils. Feel life moving through you as you quietly breathe. Try to focus only on your breath until your timer signals five minutes have elapsed.

You can extend the time you breathe like this the next day. Do it at least once every day. These mini-meditations will do wonders.

④ Take short "savoring breaks."

STOP—YOUR WORK, YOUR ERRANDS, your project, your meal, your rushing—and pause to consider the emotion you are feeling, the beauty around you, the taste of your food, the kindness someone exhibited, or the sweetness of a memory. Whatever you can focus on and savor in that moment will be a gift to yourself.

Make these "savoring breaks" a regular part of your day. Be conscious to take one at least once a day and build up to more. The breaks will be so pleasant that in time you'll be doing them frequently and without having to remind yourself.

5 **Start your day with a minute of stretching, even before you leave your bed. Then write a page in a journal.**

PICK OUT A SMALL JOURNAL and keep it by your bedside. After you first open your eyes, begin to stretch your arms and legs a bit. Extend them, reach, wiggle your fingers and toes, make some circles in the air. Then shift your shoulders, rock side-to-side, and move in any other way that feels good.

Next, start to jot in your journal. It doesn't matter what you write—just begin and see what comes up. A minute or two will do the trick, or you can spend a bit more time. This begins the day with thoughtfulness, rather than jumping right into action. It will bring more focus to your morning and, likely, your whole day.

6 **Soak in a hot bath at the end of the day.**

LIGHT CANDLES, ADD SOME SOOTHING BATH OIL into the filling tub if you like, maybe play some soothing music. Then just sink into the warmth and be quiet.

Pay attention to your senses. Feel the warm water on your skin, breathe in the scents, gaze at the flicker of the candles, tune into the subtle sounds around you. And do nothing.

BIG IDEA
Creating = Doing Something New or Different

Give yourself permission, encouragement, and space to play! Then let yourself revise your early efforts, because the ideas and outcomes may be awkward or unsatisfying at first. When you continue to experiment and shape those ideas, you are a true creator!

LIVE
IN THE
Present

I focus on what is happening NOW.

When I live focused on the current moment, I live only in the now. I avoid the stress, distraction, and wasted energy of replaying old stories. I steer clear of damaging worry and anxiety about what may lie ahead. I know that if I concern myself with things that I cannot be certain will come to pass, I suffer in advance for things that may or may not happen. And I lose the wonderful moment I am in, with all the possibilities that lie in the present moment. I refuse to suffer the huge losses that come with obsessing about the past or fearing the future.

I know that living in each moment means I appreciate all that is good in my life now. And it means I can create the best approach for me to handle what lies right in front of me. I set my direction and continue to make my next best decision in each moment.

We all sometimes find ourselves replaying painful, upsetting, or frustrating moments from the past.

Or we ruminate on things that recently happened and concern us. We often obsess about these things. When we ruminate over negative past experiences, we pull our focus away from the now and back to unhappiness. Thus we suffer more than we need to.

Of course there can be lessons learned from looking back, and lessons learned are important. But most of the rehashing we do hurts us. Once we have considered, learned helpful lessons, and gleaned insights, it's time to consciously leave those thoughts behind. Otherwise rehashing takes us away from living in the present moment and considering the opportunities we have now.

We can also spin out scenarios for what lies ahead and become fearful or anxious about things that are not happening and may never happen.

Why risk missing opportunities that are in front of you in the current moment? Why let good moments pass by unnoticed? How can you keep from diverting your attention instead of being present and considering which next step you want to create in the present moment?

1 Pay attention and recognize when you are living in the past or replaying something that upset you.

BE ALERT TO THOSE THOUGHTS. Keep a little notebook handy so that you can jot down when the thoughts showed up, if they were triggered by something in particular, and how they shifted your attention.

See if you notice that this happens when you're tired, or after conversations with particular people, or if some other event is a common trigger. If you can see patterns, you will be able to stay alert to times you're prone to slipping into "replay mode." That awareness can help you stop the replay impulse before it takes over your thoughts.

2 When you are aware that thoughts about the past are circulating, or you are playing out future scenarios, bring your attention back to your current moment.

WHERE ARE YOU NOW? What's going on now? What can you create in this moment? What next step might you take? What new idea can you come up with now?

If you make it a habit to bring the above questions to the forefront of your thoughts, you will shift out of the rehashing and fast-forwarding and into the present more easily than you may imagine. Remember that the present moment is likely to be full of wonderful possibilities.

Some people rehash and/or fast-forward as a way to avoid facing a current dilemma. If you recognize that you are doing that, consider the power you have in the present moment to contemplate your options and the choices you have. Even if none of your choices is great, remember that you always have a choice. You always have an opportunity to make your next best decision. When you are present in the moment, you are your strongest advocate. When you make deliberate choices, you are living big in the moment. You do not let opportunities pass you by!

③ Use emotions that come up, and create.

WHEN YOU FEEL TUGGED BACK to challenging thoughts or fret about what lies ahead—especially if these are persistent habits—put the negative emotions you feel to work in ways that will free you. How? It's really a lot easier than you might imagine.

Think about what poem you can write, or what you can draw to express the emotion you're feeling. What music might you play—on an instrument or by finding music that expresses your fear, anger, or frustration—and play loudly?

Use the emotions connected to the thoughts you are pulled to as the focus of whatever you choose to create.

If you feel anger or fear or are full of regret, for instance, try writing about that. You can pour your feelings onto the page, or you might write a story in which all the emotions play out in a fictitious scenario.

Try to make a drawing, or a series of drawings, to express the emotions you're feeling. If, for instance, you are angry or upset, try to draw the ugliest pictures you possibly can in order to make the feelings visual.

If you like to cook, you can vigorously chop up food with all the passion you feel in order to get the emotions out on your cutting board. (Afterwards, you can turn the ingredients into something delicious!)

Whatever you try, really go for it. When you create with the intense emotion that has shown up, you virtually "download" it. You'll feel a wonderful sense of release and relief. Amazingly, you will find that once you have used the emotion in a creative act, you can more easily leave the emotions and the thoughts that spawned them behind.

BIG IDEA

Meditation Centers You

When you find yourself fast-forwarding or replaying scenes from the past, you can meditate to quickly return to the present moment.

. . .

DOWNLOAD
a guided meditation to help you get present. Listen to it whenever you need it.
TheLiveBigBook.com/gifts

FIND ADVICE
about how to create a meditation practice, and extend it, on page 109.

LOVE
MORE

I let love flow
ABUNDANTLY.

I cultivate the magnificent force of love in my life.

The root of all loving is self-love. I must truly love and treasure myself, appreciate my magnificence, and feel deserving of love and goodness of all kinds in order to fully love others and allow love to expand into the world as it's meant to.

I know that self-love must be actively cultivated and nurtured. I start with awareness, then gently encourage self-love every day, knowing that random displays of self-love are not enough.

Just as a garden grows with ample water and sunlight, so love grows in my heart. And it radiates. I send love abundantly to those who support me and to those who bring challenges my way, knowing the power of love is enormous. It is fuel for my life.

Many people find the word "love" to be uncomfortable unless it's used to express feelings toward a close family member, friend, or a significant life partner.

Some people struggle with the word even in the closest relationships in their lives. It's often a challenge to bring the concept of love into the spheres of work and business, to those with whom we have casual relationships, and certainly to people we don't even know.

Even self-love is a challenge, with many of us linking it to selfishness, or, worse, narcissism.

The truth is that love is a magnificent force that can be embraced and brought into all of the interactions in our lives. Self-love is healthy and important—and it is an antidote to damaging self-criticism. When we believe in the beauty and power of love, and consciously feel and use it in all of our interactions, we live gloriously, abundantly, and generously. Every way we show kindness and convey love makes the world a better place. Our hearts are nourished as we nourish those of others.

The exercises that follow can help you embrace love more fully and make it a bigger part of your life.

Strengthen self-love.

THERE ARE SEVERAL EASY WAYS TO BOLSTER SELF-LOVE and start to benefit from it. When you wake up, and before bed, smile at yourself in the mirror. Set a timer for two minutes and do it right after you brush your teeth.

Simply gaze at your face and smile lovingly into your eyes. It may feel awkward, but stick with it. It will feel OK in time—in fact, better than OK! During the day, make a point of consciously focusing on feeling deserving—of special experiences, of kindness, of self-forgiveness and compassion, of everything good in the world. Treat yourself to time just for you and to small gifts or experiences that will make you smile. Simple things like taking a walk in the park or stopping in a cafe to enjoy a special new flavor of tea are small treats that build self-love.

Generate ideas for practicing self-love.

USE THIS DISCOVERY DOZEN.

"To love myself more, I can _____."

DISCOVERY **12** DOZEN

When you have written 12 different endings to your sentences, pick three of the most appealing things you wrote and begin to add those things to your life.

For instance, if you wrote and liked this sentence: *"To love myself more, I can be more physically active,"* commit to spending a few extra minutes exercising today—even if it's simply taking a longer walking route than usual to get in a bit more fresh air and movement. Or sign up to take a yoga class this week. Take action on at least three of the ideas you wrote.

Note: You can repeat this Discovery Dozen again on another day and see if interesting new ideas show up. You'll have new things to take action on. And you can always make your own Discovery Dozen sentence roots. For instance, you might try, *"Increasing self-love makes me feel _____."* Or structure a new Discovery Dozen this way: *"If I _____, I will be happier today."*

3 ## Practice "sending love," even when you are frustrated, or your impulse is to be angry or resentful.

IF PEOPLE BOTHER YOU OR DO YOU HARM, whether it's intentional or simply thoughtless, you can silently send them love rather than blaming or stewing in anger. It may sound crazy, but when you choose to say to yourself, "I send you love," you let go of anger and pain, and you send positive energy to others that they need! If you harbor resentment, you only hurt yourself.

You may need to practice this before it becomes a habit. When you become accustomed to sending love to the person who cut you off in traffic, or played office politics in a way that impacted you negatively, or to someone who was too self-absorbed to see that they were unkind, you will experience a shift in your heart. Love will fill the space that resentment and anger used to take up. You will feel more at peace. In time, you may see positive changes in the people to whom you directed loving thoughts.

Send a short note of love and appreciation to someone.

EXPRESS LOVE IN VISIBLE and clear ways whenever you can. One nice way to do that is to write a note to someone who did something kind for you. The note can be for something significant, or for something small that would typically go unacknowledged. Your note will deliver love to the recipient and make that person aware that their kindness was felt and appreciated. (And writing your note by hand on note paper or a pretty card will make the sentiments even more special for the recipient.)

Or you might buy a small item for someone and simply tell them you thought of them when you saw it (whether it's a pretty stone found on a beach, a treat from a bakery, a small scented candle, or a box of lovely tea).

Notice how these small expressions of love rebound and expand in beautiful ways.

BE
TRUE
TO
YOUR

I trust my
HEART.

My heart holds my deepest beliefs and my true passions. There is only truth there, and it's the most important truth I have.

The key to living that truth begins with connecting to what I hold in my heart. I have opened my heart and found those treasures, to truly know myself.

When I sensed pain in that precious spot, it used to make me afraid—and that paralyzed me for a time. I built walls around my heart, believing the walls protected me from the pain. But I learned that I could open my heart without fear.

And my heart was desperate to be opened, examined, known. When I did that, and discovered its bounty, I began to live in alignment with—and guided by—my truth. I started to truly live big.

For many people, it seems mysterious, or even out of reach, to connect to the truth that lies in their hearts.

But it is possible. There need not be fear, though you may find you need to test the waters to truly believe that it will be achievable and comfortable. The exercises on these pages will help you feel safe as you mine your heart for the truths that lie there.

You can open your heart in many wonderful ways. See which of these techniques you most enjoy.

1 ## Journaling.

START TO MAKE A FREQUENT PRACTICE OF WRITING—even
if you typically don't write much, or think you are not a "good writer."
This writing is only for your eyes.

Try to do a little free writing when you first awaken, and see what
shows up on the pages. Forget punctuation and grammar—just write,
without any self-editing. Let whatever thoughts come to mind land on
your page. Ramble. These words are yours, they come from inside of
you. You may find that surprises and insights show up quickly, or you
may need to write for many days before you discover interesting things
of which you were not conscious. Be patient with this process and relax
into it. Over time, you will find truths, and clarity will emerge.

2 ## Do a bit of writing using "writing prompts."

WHEN YOU START WITH A PROMPT, you have a jumping-in point
for writing, and some prompts will lead you to especially interesting
and revealing discoveries. After reading a prompt, you can write a page
or two, or more. It's up to you.

Write whatever comes to mind based on the prompt. Take a few
minutes to do this with various prompts several times over the next
few days (at breakfast, on your lunch break, or on a quiet midday break)
and see what comes up for you.

Here are a few prompts to start with. Pick one that appeals to you, then try another one at some other time. Just pick one and start writing whatever comes into your mind.

- *The deep recesses of my heart are sending me a message.*
- *Now's time to make a little dream come true.*
- *The child inside me can come alive at any age and at any time.*
- *Sometimes anger is the path to freedom.*
- *It's risky to live a life without risks.*
- *My old stories are waiting to be rewritten.*

After you use some of these prompts and get the hang of this exercise, make up your own prompts. Be provocative and creative! Then make a date with yourself to write with a prompt at least twice a week.

3 **Complete a few different Discovery Dozen sentences.**

DISCOVERY DOZENS LIKE THESE can unearth what's waiting to be discovered in your heart:

"Right now, my heart wants me to know _____."
"Right now, I have a huge urge to _____."
"Deep in my heart, I know _____."
"My heart tells me that no matter what other people (or my mother/ my boss/my friend/my kids) think or say, _____."

Do a Discovery Dozen at least three times this week. You can repeat the same sentence root on different days and see what new things emerge at different times, or choose new ones each time.

I encourage you to make up your own Discovery Dozens too. Use your imagination and be playful with them.

4 Expand the Discovery Dozen process.

THERE'S ANOTHER GREAT THING TO DO in order to make even more discoveries with a Discovery Dozen. You can take some of the answers you wrote and go deeper with some of the ideas by using them as a starting point for new Discovery Dozen sentences.

For example, you might have completed one of the Discovery Dozens above with something like this:

"Right now, I have a huge urge to travel to Asia and experience the culture there."

You can take that thought and make a new sentence root that goes like this:

"I want to travel to Asia and experience the culture there because _____."

See what your new Discovery Dozen reveals to you when you begin with that root.

This variation would work well too:

"If I travel to Asia and experience the culture, I may discover _____."

You can always delve deeper by making up new Discovery Dozens like these when you want to explore more about something that intrigues you in your first set of sentences. Try it out and see what discoveries are waiting in your heart, ready to come into the light.

FEEL

free

Feeling **FREE** ensures that I am free.

I can truly be free when my spirit soars— which it does when I'm connected to my passion and the authentic purpose I know is mine to pursue.

Freedom comes naturally when there's clarity in my life. I actively seek clarity about what I want. My truth emerges when I create. Through open expression, painting with colors, I tap my heart. Through writing, letting my thoughts pour out intuitively, I open my heart. I connect to my truth and keep going. Clarity continues to unfold as I continue to create.

When I feel a clear connection to my heart and my purpose, I soar. I feel fantastically free, and I truly am free.

The idea of what it can mean to feel free is very personal. It may strike you in many ways.

Do you yearn to freely express yourself? To freely create? To keep the self-critical voice in your head at bay? To stop doubt from being an impediment? To be free of fear?

Do you want to feel free to pursue adventures? Meet new people? Make changes? Do more meaningful work?

Do you yearn to feel free so you can stop living small, in whatever way that limits your life?

You can find clarity and freedom about all of those things. You can begin to create as a way to get to deeper levels of insight, understanding yourself, connecting to what your heart yearns for and to passions that excite you.

1 Define what "feeling free" means to you.

BEGIN WITH MINING WHAT'S IN YOUR HEART.

DISCOVERY
12
DOZEN

Discover what makes your spirit soar, or what would make it
soar (or soar higher). Ask yourself about the kind of ease and freedom
you yearn for.

The Discovery Dozen is a great tool for this inquiry. You can use these
sentence roots or create variations of your own.

"To feel truly free, I (need to/must/want to/will) _____ ."
"I have a huge desire/a burning passion to _____ ."
"My heart would soar if _____ ."

Or you might prefer this variation:

"My heart soars when _____ ."

Another way to explore this question is to jump ahead and use exercise
#2 in "Speak Your Truth" (on page 79). You'll see that the exercise is
done with a partner. Be sure to choose someone you trust and with
whom you feel safe to say everything and anything that arises as you
are repeatedly asked, "What do you want?" If you trust the process and
go deep, you will hit gold.

Bear in mind, too, that the question of what it means to you to feel
free is big and important, and your answers may change over time.
Explore your definitions for how you want to feel free now and revisit

this inquiry as your life evolves. As you create more freedom around things that limit you now, new levels of freedom will be ready for you to pursue.

② Get your spirit soaring!

THE OUTCOME OF YOUR EXPLORATION in exercise #1 may have revealed a huge desire around one thing, or you may have identified a number of ways you yearn to feel free and are ready to take steps to realize that freedom. Gaining understanding is always important before moving into action, so that the action you embark on will be focused and productive. But actually getting started on your path to feeling free may feel daunting, or you may feel unsure about how to get things rolling.

This is where your innate creativity can be tapped. Think about the ways you can begin to try out the freedom you desire.

For instance, if you yearn to feel free to connect with people when you are at events filled with strangers, think about an opening line that will help you start a warm conversation. You might stand near the door, see someone else standing alone, and then say, "You look like you're waiting to spot a familiar face, like I am. Hi, I'm Nancy. What brings you here this evening?" If you try it out, there's a very good chance you'll spend a few pleasant minutes chatting, and you may discover you have something interesting in common. The next time, you'll feel freer to initiate a relaxed conversation. In time, you'll be at ease and will welcome new encounters.

How many ideas for small steps can you create to experience and get comfortable with the new ways you want to feel and be free? Make a list, then make a point of using your ideas. Trust that small steps are doable and will have an impact. You'll have opportunities to get comfortable with the range of feelings that will arise when you make the effort, and you'll start feeling freer as you stay with it.

Accelerate the process by creating.

ACTIVELY CREATING WILL SPEED YOUR PROCESS of feeling free, no matter what kind of freedom you are working to open.

There is enormous flow when you create, so make it part of the rhythm of your life. Whether you choose to write freely upon waking, take music lessons, or join a class to sculpt, any way that you create will work wonders.

This is an opportunity to be courageous and to create in new and inventive ways. Be willing—and free—to try new things. If something doesn't feel right, no harm, no foul. Go on to the next!

Share the ways you are bringing freedom into your life.

AS YOUR FREEDOM EXPANDS, enjoy sharing your experiences. You might start writing a blog. You might invite others to join you. The sharing will keep your efforts alive and expanding—and you'll be giving the gift of inspiration as you share.

Continue to expand and elevate freedom of every kind.

WITH SOME MOMENTUM IN PLACE, you can envision audacious ways of being free and reaching new heights. Ask yourself: If nothing were impossible, what would I do? Put a date on your calendar on the first of each month to check in with yourself, ask that question, and then start taking small steps toward your vision.

Live
WITHOUT
Fear

I conquered
fear to THRIVE.

Fear had paralyzed me. It limited huge potential, impacted everything, and diminished my world.

Why is fear so pervasive? Not because of a lot of danger. Danger is very real, and when there's danger, fear is an automatic, crucial response.

But fear was often my choice in the absence of danger. I feared powerful emotions and coping with them, so I left them unexplored and painful. I feared failure, so I did not play, experiment, or risk making mistakes. Sometimes I feared success and held myself back from possibilities that were well within my capabilities.

I learned to safely transform my emotions through creativity. I recognized and quieted my damaging self-critic. I built self-love and believed I was deserving of my dreams. Now I live without fear.

Everyone experiences fear—even the most courageous people we can think of. But they know how to cope with it.

Unfounded fear may be the factor that most limits happiness and potential. The impact is devastating when we live with fear as a driver.

It's easy to see that fear is prevalent all around us. Advertisers use fear to persuade us, politicians endlessly prey on fear, and most work environments are rife with fear. Parents even employ fear in attempts to teach better behavior—believing it's a positive way to raise their children. We absorb the negative emotional energy of all of that fear without realizing it, and our self-critics have a field day with it. We become worriers. We are so afraid of failing that we don't experiment, play, or dare to test our ideas.

Whether it inhibits us from working through an important personal or professional issue or paralyzes us completely, fear is one damaging emotion when we don't find ways to dispel it.

TRY THESE
EXERCISES
TO COPE
WITH AND
CONQUER
FEAR

Identify fear that you may not be aware of.

IF YOU FEEL A SENSATION THAT YOU KNOW IS FEAR, or think might be, try this Discovery Dozen to "diagnose" what's bothering you:

"My biggest fear right now is _____."

After you've completed the Discovery Dozen, do two more rounds of sentence completions.

Start by picking the three answers you think are the most irrational fears on your list. For each of the three, do a second Discovery Dozen, like this:

"Instead of being worried, I can _____ when I am afraid of [sinking in quicksand—or whatever irrational fear you picked]."

You'll likely see that there are lots of easy ways to dispel your irrational fears.

Next, select three of the answers from your first Discovery Dozen that you think may be the most valid of your fears. For each, complete this sentence 12 times:

"Instead of being afraid [I will get bad news from the doctor—or whatever you picked], right now I can switch to _____."

Your answers could be things like: thinking about beautiful weather, cooking a big pot of healthy soup, turning up the volume of my favorite song and dancing away the tension, or calling my best friend and making a date to watch a funny movie.

This kind of self-prompting will inspire you to take action that will help you cope with your fears when you feel them, so you can shake off the paralysis and move forward.

2 Choose to play!

WHEN WE PLAY AND LAUGH, we free up energy. Getting silly lets our bodies relax. In that state of mind (and body), fear has a tough time persisting.

Play is a great way to keep fear at bay, and it's also something you can do whether fear is just beginning to creep in or has already got you in its clutches. Give yourself permission to play in any number of ways. If children are around, you're in luck. They are naturals at play of all sorts and will gladly welcome you as a partner. Play with adults, too—go bowling, play a game of tag football or a round of charades, or see who can create the craziest yummy sandwich. The possibilities are endless if you use your imagination.

Even on your own, there are great ways to play. If you're driving, take a little time to purposely get lost and see what you discover. Take a walk with a camera in hand and see what surprising things and unusual compositions you can capture. Delight yourself!

Any way you let yourself play will not only dispel fear, but bring you a bonus. Play prompts your intuitive right brain to open up and generate new ideas and new ways of thinking about all sorts of things.

③ Take small risks.

TRY TAKING A SMALL RISK once or twice a week. See how it feels, and see what happens.

Your "small risk" might be to do something unfamiliar, cook something tricky, or ask for help from a stranger.

The outcome may be a lovely surprise, or simply be fine. And if something unpleasant happens, you'll have the chance to learn from it, laugh at it, or recognize your own resilience and move on. After you get comfortable taking small risks, you'll feel better about taking bigger risks, without fear.

④ Transform fear through creativity.

CREATING IN EVERY WAY IMAGINABLE is a powerful antidote to fear. Rather than let fear fester inside, you can put it to work constructively. Here's the way it works.

Choose to create when you feel fear! Fear can be fuel for any creative act.

You might pound on clay or deliberately make a series of hideous drawings. Play air guitar to heavy metal music. You might write a letter to the person your fear is related to, or create a story with all the drama you feel. Any kind of creativity, fueled by your fearful emotions, will transform your fear as you create.

If the fear is stubborn, keep at it, or change up your approach and keep going. The more you create with the energy, the more you'll release the fear.

You will open yourself to amazing possibilities. As you are able to take new action, don't be surprised to experience magic in your life!

ALIGN WITH YOUR PURPOSE

My purpose is my COMPASS.

Finding the purpose I was meant to live took time. I was asked to work in a family business, but my heart said "no" to that idea. I was fortunate to find a field that excited me and supported me, but, after several decades, I realized that my work was not truly fulfilling. My heart yearned for something else, something more meaningful.

Discovering my purpose came from truly knowing and honoring myself. The process was fueled by self-love. I realized that mining my heart to identify my deepest desires was the key to finding a direction that would impact the world. It was worth the effort to pursue the process and dive into preparing to do my new work. A richly satisfying and meaningful life has been my reward.

Are you among the masses of people who find themselves doing work that does not feel aligned with their true purpose?

Did you follow a path your family wanted for you? Did you take a first job and find yourself in a field that you later realized you did not really love? Do you have a role that doesn't bring you joy?

Do you feel dissatisfaction, but don't know how to connect to your real purpose? Do you feel like you're too old to make a change, or too advanced in your field to shift directions? Maybe you know what you'd love to do, but feel that it's not a realistic path for you to pursue?

Take the time to discover what has deep meaning for you—what you will be excited to wake up to each day. Or, if you know what that is, believe in the possibilities to create the future you desire. If a career shift seems impossible, consider how you can make an avocation of that desire, or a volunteer activity centered on it. Making your purpose a part of your everyday life will bring you huge fulfillment.

Uncover — or reconnect to — your purpose.

THE DISCOVERY DOZEN IS A GREAT TOOL for self-discovery.
Try completing one, two, or all of these sentences with
12 answers:

*"If I could spend my days doing anything, I'd love to
_____ ."*

"When I think of making my work _____, my heart soars."
"My deepest satisfaction comes from _____ ."

Even if good answers emerge on the first try, you may want to repeat
the exercise a few times this week and next. On different days, in
different frames of mind, you may make new discoveries. Over
time, your answers will likely start to include related or repeated
ideas, providing you with excellent insights. Or you may have clear
validation of a direction you've longed to pursue and had set aside
up to now.

Create opportunities for discovery.

AFTER YOU DO THE DISCOVERY DOZENS, you may find you've
touched on interesting ideas, but feel that none stand out as the
purpose you think is "it." In that case, you may feel frustration.
The key is to be ready for the answer to show up in your life. And for
that to happen, your heart must be open and ready to connect to your

"next." What does that mean? And how can that happen?

Start by consciously deciding to keep an open mind. Be actively curious and be willing to follow your intuition. Stop any negative self-talk that shows up. (That's your self-critic, and it's comfortable with the status quo. It will try to sabotage your efforts, so be alert to it. When you hear those negative thoughts, you can firmly but lovingly tell your self-critic it's not needed and to get out of the way for a while.)

When you are in an open state of mind, new doors will appear, and you will notice them. You can then open those doors and explore.

❸ Dive in! Experience the new possibilities.

WHEN YOU FEEL READY to explore the direction or directions you feel could be your true purpose—or if you know you've hit on "it" but are not sure what to do next—there are great ways to test new waters.

Look for classes that you can take that are related to your interests. You might take a course on investing, or register for a painting class, or find a culinary course that will let you both experience that type of work and learn more about it. Doing so will also put you in contact with people in the field you want to explore. The connections you can make offer great opportunities to ask your burning questions and will introduce you to new and deeper levels of understanding—not to mention, offer you the chance to be introduced to people who can become valuable resources for you as you take steps to move into a new arena.

This process may feel somewhat intimidating, so if you find yourself feeling reluctance or hesitation, fuel yourself with lots of self-loving thoughts and then think about taking these steps as a game. You have the chance to explore without making a long-term commitment. Enjoy the process! Let yourself feel adventurous and playful. The more upbeat the energy and the more enthusiastic the curiosity you can bring to this process, the more you will be able to connect to what resonates deeply for you. You will know if something is interesting, but not as exciting as you'd expected, and you'll know when you have found your "sweet spot."

From there, you can begin to create a vision of the future you desire and begin to take steps to create that reality. You need not hurry. You can continue to learn and meet with people who will provide you with guidance, advice, and insights you need to make the decisions that are right for you, one step at a time.

Find people who will support you as you continue through this big process and help you celebrate each step you take on your path. Having supportive people in your life who see your vision and want to help you reach it will be a huge asset. Remind yourself that you don't have to do it all on your own.

Remember to keep connected to the joy of it as you continue. This is living big!

B

E

P A

T I

E N

T

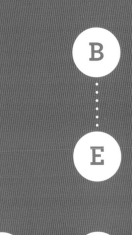

Patience is a GIFT to myself.

I have always been naturally enthusiastic and eager to get answers, find solutions, have experiences, and make progress.

When I slow down, get quiet, and find more focus in my life, I find it easier to be patient and trust that things will happen when they are meant to. If something has not happened as I've wished, I can simply say, "It has not happened yet."

I trust—and know—that whatever happens, when it happens, I will be fine. I will rejoice, or I will make a decision, or I will adjust to a new situation.

I know that my life is flowing and unfolding as it should. I am able to be patient and ready to receive what comes when it arrives.

The prevalence of impatience in individual people, and in our culture at large, is remarkable.

We are not content to wait—for almost anything! We want fast food, instant gratification, speedy answers to our questions, and short lines in the stores we frequent. We speed along highways, distracted, and rarely see anything other than a blur around us.

We don't know what to do with ourselves when we have to wait.

This lack of patience is exacerbated by the crazy pace we have made normal in our lives. We rush all day long, we barely stop to eat lunch, and we overcommit and have more on our calendars than we can reasonably do. This frantic pace of life makes it almost impossible to find patience, and that hinders all sorts of happiness. When we impatiently snap at a co-worker—or, worse, our children—we are not the people we want to be. We yearn to have more patience, but don't know how to get to it.

TRY THESE
EXERCISES
TO BUILD
YOUR
ABILITY TO
BE PATIENT

1 Start with why.

AS SIMON SINEK BRILLIANTLY BROUGHT TO LIGHT in his TED talk and book, *Start with Why*, knowing why we do things is crucial. This is a perfect time to explore why you desire more patience in your life—as well as why it's such a struggle for you to be patient. This Discovery Dozen is a great tool to help you find your answers.

Begin by completing this sentence 12 times:

"I wish I could be more patient because _____ ."

Your answers might be things like, *"I wish I could be more patient because I hate feeling the stress that comes with waiting,"* or, *"... I drive myself crazy when things take a long time to resolve,"* or, *"... when I am on edge with impatience, it triggers arguments with my partner."*

Now complete this sentence:

"It's challenging for me to be patient when _____ ."

Circle a few of the answers that stand out for you and complete another Discovery Dozen with this sentence:

"At those times, it's hard to be patient because _____ ."

You are now likely to have clearer insights. Be loving toward yourself for embarking on this exploration. You can use what you have learned to begin to make change.

2 **Envision what patience will look like for you.**

AFTER EXPLORING AND REFLECTING on the insights
revealed in your answers to the Discovery Dozen
sentences in exercise #1, you can move on to imagining
how being more patient might impact your life. This is important,
because when we have a vision of something we want, we are more
motivated and able to change entrenched habits that no longer serve
us. Start by completing these sentences.

"If I had more patience, I would _____*."*
Your answers might include, *"be relieved!"* or, *"my blood pressure
would go down."*

"To feel OK about things happening more slowly, I can _____*."*
Your answers here might be things like *"stop fast-forwarding to worst-
case scenarios",* or *"remember that I was resilient and more motivated
the last time I got a bad mark on an exam."*

"When I learn to be more patient, _____*."*
Your answers this time might include, *"I'll be more relaxed,"* or *"I'll
enjoy being calmer."*

When you begin to create a concrete vision of yourself as a more
patient person, and trust in yourself to cope with the feelings that
come up as you wait, you'll be laying the groundwork for big change.

3 **Learn to pay careful attention.**

NOW THAT YOU ARE MOTIVATED to slow down and allow
yourself to be patient, you'll need to be alert to the signals you have
become habituated to when you slide into impatience. To catch
yourself and head off impatient responses, you need to think about
the specific thoughts that you're prone to having.

This is the time to pay attention to the impulse you have to think things like, *"When will that email arrive with the news I am waiting for?"* When you are alert to thinking that way, you can consciously prompt yourself to reframe those thoughts. You might say to yourself, *"I know he said he'd email me today, but he probably doesn't have an answer yet. I am eager to hear the news and trust that he'll write when the information is available."* After giving it some time, you can certainly send an inquiry about the matter at hand, but you will be able to write a note simply asking for a quick update—one that does not convey anxiety, only interest.

BIG IDEA

Find a Quiet Spot to Sit and Meditate

Meditation is a gift you can give yourself when you seek patience—or any time.

. . .

DOWNLOAD
a special guided meditation to help you find patience:
TheLiveBigBook.com/gifts

READ
about how to create a meditation practice on page 109.

Believe in your ability to change.

YOU HAVE WORKED THROUGH a thoughtful process and tested ways to build and practice patience. It may take a while, so it's important to remind yourself that you can actually make this change. Pay attention to your self-talk—both self-critical talk and ways you tend to slide back into impatient thinking. Regularly remind yourself to trust both yourself and the universe around you. Remember to stay calm and to feel at peace. You might ask someone to be an "accountability buddy" you can turn to for support and who will help you stay on track.

BE

Grateful

GRATITUDE

enriches my life.

When times are calm or impacted by stress, I never lose sight of all there is for which to be grateful. I tune my heart and mind to all of the blessings in my life. I am grateful for the small things that lie in tiny crevices as I move through my day.

I feel gratitude that my body is able to stretch in yoga class—as well as for the smiles of the people around me. I feel grateful when my child is excited about what he learned in school. I am grateful for the tastes and textures of fresh fruits and delicate cheeses, and for the person who held a door open for me. I feel grateful for each breeze on a hot day.

Sustaining a focus on gratitude increases my vitality. It enhances my relationships, helps me to be more resilient, and adds joy to my life.

I love that the concept of gratitude is spoken of so much these days.

It wasn't long ago that I never heard people considering the gift of gratitude. It truly is powerful.

If this idea is something you've laughed at or haven't thought about much, or if your "gratitude practice" is spotty and not a regular part of your daily mindset, there's a big opportunity waiting for you as you bring more focus on gratitude into your life.

Even those who are currently mindful of gratitude can benefit from having more ways to consider and enhance the role of being grateful to have a richer, more resilient life.

1 Learn about and experience how gratitude can impact you.

WHEN WE MAKE AN EFFORT TO UNDERSTAND something we have an interest in or have curiosity about, we are better able to embrace it. Lots of people think being grateful sounds nice, but question whether "practicing it" is worthwhile. Here is a simple way you can better understand the power of gratitude.

Think about something that challenges you. For instance, maybe you have a close friend who is ill and you are distressed. Maybe you are unhappy at work. Reflect on how you typically feel when this matter is in the front of your mind—or how it's striking you right now. How do you respond?

Are you anxious? Do you feel frustrated or angry? Can you feel the emotion resonating in your body when you pay attention to your response? Emotions like fear, frustration, worry, anger, jealousy, bitterness, anxiety, and more come up often for all of us. And how we respond to them impacts not only our mood and attitudes and behaviors, but our physical health too.

See how things shift when you try this little process.

Get out a paper and a pen. As you think about that challenge again, and feel the emotion that comes up, pause, breathe, and jot down 12 things for which you are grateful—in spite of the challenge.

These can be things as big as the fact that your kids are happy and thriving at school, or as small as the sight of beautiful clouds out a window. Put anything on the list that comes to mind (and list more than 12 things if you want).

Now pause to breathe again, and then quietly and slowly read your list. Connect to the emotions you sense in your body as you consider the things for which you expressed gratitude.

Do you feel a physical difference? Did your stressed thoughts shift? Has your impulse to do something as a response changed?

Researchers have documented the power of gratitude practiced on a daily basis, and the findings are fantastic. Making a list of as few as five things for which you are grateful every morning (or evening, or over lunch) can help you face even overwhelming challenges and find balance, hope, and the ability to cope with anything in your life.

Things that have been observed by researchers studying people who kept a gratitude journal include:

- ► boosts in productivity and mood
- ► more alertness, enthusiasm, and determination
- ► markedly reduced stress (27 percent less)
- ► improved health and sleep, and better relationships
- ► stronger immune systems, reduced anxiety and/or depression
- ► more happiness

Who doesn't want some or all of those things?

2 Adopt more ways to build a practice of gratitude.

NOW THAT YOU HAVE TRIED WRITING a gratitude list and have a greater understanding of the benefits of cultivating gratitude, it's time to think about expanding it and finding ways you can make a regular gratitude practice a reality. Consider these approaches.

First, look back at the list of 12 things you wrote and, next to each one, add why you're grateful for it. This will help you gain more insight.

Then think about mechanics. If a bedside journal for morning or evening lists doesn't appeal to you—or even if it does and you want more ways to practice gratitude—tuck a small notebook into your bag, briefcase, or pocket. If it's handy, you'll more easily pull it out in the moment to note things that come to mind on the fly. After all, by the end of the day you may have forgotten a sweet observation made as you were on your way to a meeting or something notable that came up in a casual conversation.

Having a small gratitude journal on hand is especially good for the times you find yourself feeling difficult emotions. You can easily pull it out, take a breath, and focus on what you are grateful for to dispel the tension. It's a portable, easy way to find relief and comfort. In no time, you will have pages of things for which you are grateful that you can flip through and reflect on.

You may want to choose a journal that looks distinctive. That way, when you see it, you'll get a visual cue to use it. The journal can be an inexpensive drugstore item or something a bit more "special." Whatever works for you is great.

Commit to a regular gratitude practice.

NOW IT'S TIME TO MAKE THIS A RITUAL IN YOUR LIFE. Take a week to experience this, then make a commitment to yourself to stick with what you like most.

See WONDER

I notice and feel MAGIC around me.

We live in an amazing world. Breathtaking vistas and exquisite sunsets are a marvel. But there's so much more that I used to miss as I rushed through my days, incessantly checked email, and grabbed lunch on the run. I missed an enormous amount of beauty in my life.

When I tune in to all of the wonder around me, life is enriched and I am inspired. The textures of flowers I see on a walk fill me with awe about nature. Smiling at the innocence of a young child with her parent connects me to a part of myself I have not thought about in ages. When I taste a new vegetable, I delight in its texture and flavor. When I hear a new melody, I am filled with emotion.

The wonders of the world are countless, but we rarely take in a fraction of what's around us that can touch our hearts and bring light and joy to our lives.

We've come back to where we began in this section, the BEING of living big: slowing down. If we are in constant motion, we cannot take note of much more than the most obvious of wonders, like a gorgeous view smack dab in front of us.

When we go slowly, pause to stop, look and notice, and then reflect, our lives are enriched as we are filled with wonder. The tiniest crack in the pavement may have a delicate flower poking up. That observation can be a momentary gift—but only if we slow down and tune our awareness to the world around us.

When we regularly take in the wonders in our midst, we fill our hearts with beauty, amazement, and delight. Our outlook on life is buoyed. Challenges feel less daunting as our spirits are lifted. We radiate joyous energy, and it is felt by everyone around us. That's a contagion we can all enjoy spreading.

Sharpen awareness.

THERE'S MUCH TO BE GAINED when you make a decision to tune your awareness in a particular way. You can tune your awareness to subtle cues from your body, like noticing which actions tend to stress a particular muscle, or noticing when you are satiated and realizing that you're still eating because the people around you are eating. You can tune your awareness to the emotions of people around you. And you can tune your awareness to the beauty and quirkiness and delights that surround you in almost any moment—if you decide to slow down and take note.

Every day for the next week, try to consciously notice new things that bring little moments of delight. See if this is a new habit you can adopt easily, or if it takes you somewhat longer to regularly take note of things like the back and forth calling of unusual songbirds, the interesting shop window with a distinctive seasonal display, the smells emanating from a bakery, the vintage sign on the side of an old industrial building, or the sidewalk chalk drawings of little children.

Enjoy recording your discoveries.

YOU CAN EXTEND THE BENEFITS OF AWARENESS. When you make lovely observations, the momentary benefits you enjoy from your observations of wonder can be enhanced when you capture them in interesting ways.

Jot notes about what you've observed, including why something caught your eye and how that moment touched your heart. If memories show up that are related to what you saw, you may want to record and reflect on them. Write about new ideas they inspired too. That's a special benefit of noticing wonder.

Perhaps you'll want to start a "wonder journal," in addition to your gratitude journal, to keep these musings collected and available for review. When you hit a moment of doubt or sadness, you can open the journal and reconnect to what brought you joy.

Another great way to capture and relive moments when you are struck by wonder is to start snapping photos of vignettes that pique your interest, items or events that delight and surprise you, or places that are so striking you'll want to see them again and again. With a smartphone in hand, this is incredibly easy to do. And it's a fantastic way to share what you saw, so that others can find pleasure as well. Whether you hold your photos close or post them on social media, it's great to keep a sharp eye out for things that most people might never notice, or never see as you do.

3 Explore the possibilities.

EVEN IF YOU'RE FINDING IT FUN and easy to notice wonder around you, there are likely places and things you might not be considering where you can find a treasure trove of unexpected amazement. Try this Discovery Dozen to see what

DISCOVERY 12 DOZEN

new ideas you can explore to make this practice an even richer one in your life.

"A surprising place I might see wonder is _____."

Complete this sentence writing as fast as you can. Let yourself be crazy and free with your answers. Exaggerate. Play. See what shows up on your list.

While *"Antarctica"* may not be realistic, if you wrote *"a junkyard,"* think about the fun of poking around a junkyard to find wonderful bits of old cars, or seeing colors and juxtapositions of things that would make fabulous photographs.

Prompting yourself to seek out wonder will broaden the scope of what you'll observe and can bring bright new joy to each day.

Invite others to share the experience.

YOU CAN CREATE SOCIAL ACTIVITIES with your partner or spouse, with a close friend, or with a whole group of people by suggesting you all go out on wonder expeditions. The "expedition" could be as simple as setting a point that's a 10-minute walk from where you are, or it could be a destination, like the beach. You might pick a theme for the excursion, such as young kids, or food, or music. Create as many interesting opportunities to share the experience with others as you can dream up.

You may even want to tell your companions how you have made this a special part of your life and prompt them to adopt it too.

THE DOING OF LIVING BIG

When we are fully present human beings,
the actions we take are essential to living big.
What will you do today to live big?

LISTEN TO YOUR INTUIT!ON

My intuition is my
SIXTH SENSE.

Some lessons take time to learn. For a long time, I resisted trusting the messages my gut sent me. I was too busy to connect to those messages, which were often "red flags." On many occasions, I talked myself into rationalizing, into taking a different path than the one my gut urged me to follow.

Then I reflected and realized the problematic consequences of that disregard. I decided it was time to stop repeating those mistakes.

Now I finely tune to the messages my gut sends me from my intuition. While loud messages are pretty easy to hear, I listen, too, to whispers of truth. I appreciate and respect the wisdom I receive from that source. I know those messages provide the most trustworthy guidance I receive.

In our data-driven, logic-focused world, the "left brain" has long been considered the trusted source for, and the preferred path to, sound decision-making.

Happily, researchers have recently been validating the power and importance of our intuitive capabilities and confirming that our right brains deserve great respect.

Still, for many who are accustomed to looking at facts and data for comfort when they consider how to make decisions, or generate ideas for their businesses or lives, it's not easy to trust their intuition—or even to sense what it's signaling to them.

We can cultivate our ability to listen to our guts—to hear the messages that our intuition sends us. We can learn to believe in the wisdom that begins in our right brains and is then infused in our bodies. We can practice listening—and trust that our intuition is sending us valuable signals (rather than habitually overriding them with "logical" thinking).

Set the stage to ignite your intuition, then listen.

WITH PRACTICE, YOU WILL HEAR YOUR INTUITION loud and clear, but you first need to create the right conditions for your intuition to get into gear and flow with ease. When you most need a creative idea or an answer to a pressing challenge, the tendency is to try and think hard, believing that's how to get to the big idea you need. Ironically, the more you try to force those ideas to emerge, the more frustrated you are likely to become. You simply cannot force your intuition to generate great ideas and answers on demand. You have to provide it with the right conditions.

Happily, it's easy to do that. Simply step away from your desk and the issue you are struggling with and do not think for a while! If you take a walk, stare out the window, wash the dishes, take a nap, or let yourself daydream, your right brain will have space to play with the data generated by your logical left brain. Before long, new ideas will show up.

Letting yourself be quiet will let you hear whispers of insight that you are unlikely to notice if you are habitually rushed and distracted. You can try it out like this: After a meeting, sit quietly for a few minutes to see if you can pick up on your own gut reactions to the people you met with, the dynamics of the discussion, and/or the ideas that were discussed. Take note of those feelings and honor them. Even if you're not sure about them when you consider them logically, try your best to trust that they will guide you well. In time, you are likely to see they were on target.

② Pay attention to subtle signals.

SOMETIMES YOUR INTUITION will give you a huge "AHA" idea. Often, however, meaningful signals will show up less noticeably. It can take practice to pick up on the subtle signals from your intuition.

To cultivate your sensitivity to those quieter signals, try some of these Discovery Dozens to see what you can tune into at any given time. You might use these prompts after a particular interaction or experience, when you sense something gnawing at you, or simply to check in with yourself.

"Right now, I hear my gut telling me _____ ."
"As I stop and listen, I have the feeling that _____ ."
"I have the distinct sense that _____ ."
"The tightness I feel in my body is telling me _____ ."

Write down anything that comes to mind, even if it seems preposterous. In fact, let yourself be as free as you can, writing whatever enters your mind. When you read through your 12 completions, you're likely going to spot some things that stand out to you as meaningful insights. If you don't come up with much, do not be concerned. You may be testing this at a time when your intuition doesn't have a lot to tell you.

③ Seek out intuitive whispers.

TO SHARPEN YOUR LISTENING SKILLS when it comes to your intuition, you can make a game of asking yourself questions. Rather than completing the following sentences 12 times, see what one answer comes to you in the moment and finish each of them. You can make up others too—have fun with this.

"If I were to start drawing right now, I have an urge to reach for the color _____."

"The stranger sitting next to me now makes me feel _____."

"I have a feeling it would be fun to _____."

"The flavor I most want to taste right now is _____."

"I sense that the person I just met is afraid of _____."

"I feel excited about the possibility that _____."

Be sure to be spontaneous and write down the first thing that pops into your mind. That's your intuition speaking!

④ Give yourself reminders.

ENJOY MAKING SOME COLORFUL SIGNS to post where you will see them often—on your bulletin board, on a wall across from your desk, or on small cards to keep in your pockets. One of them might say, *"Listen to your gut."* One might say, *"Trust your gut."* You can even get sassy and make signs that say, *"Don't fall for all that logic!"* or *"Stop overthinking when your intuition is talking to you."*

These prompts will remind you to stay tuned in to the important messages your intuition sends to you.

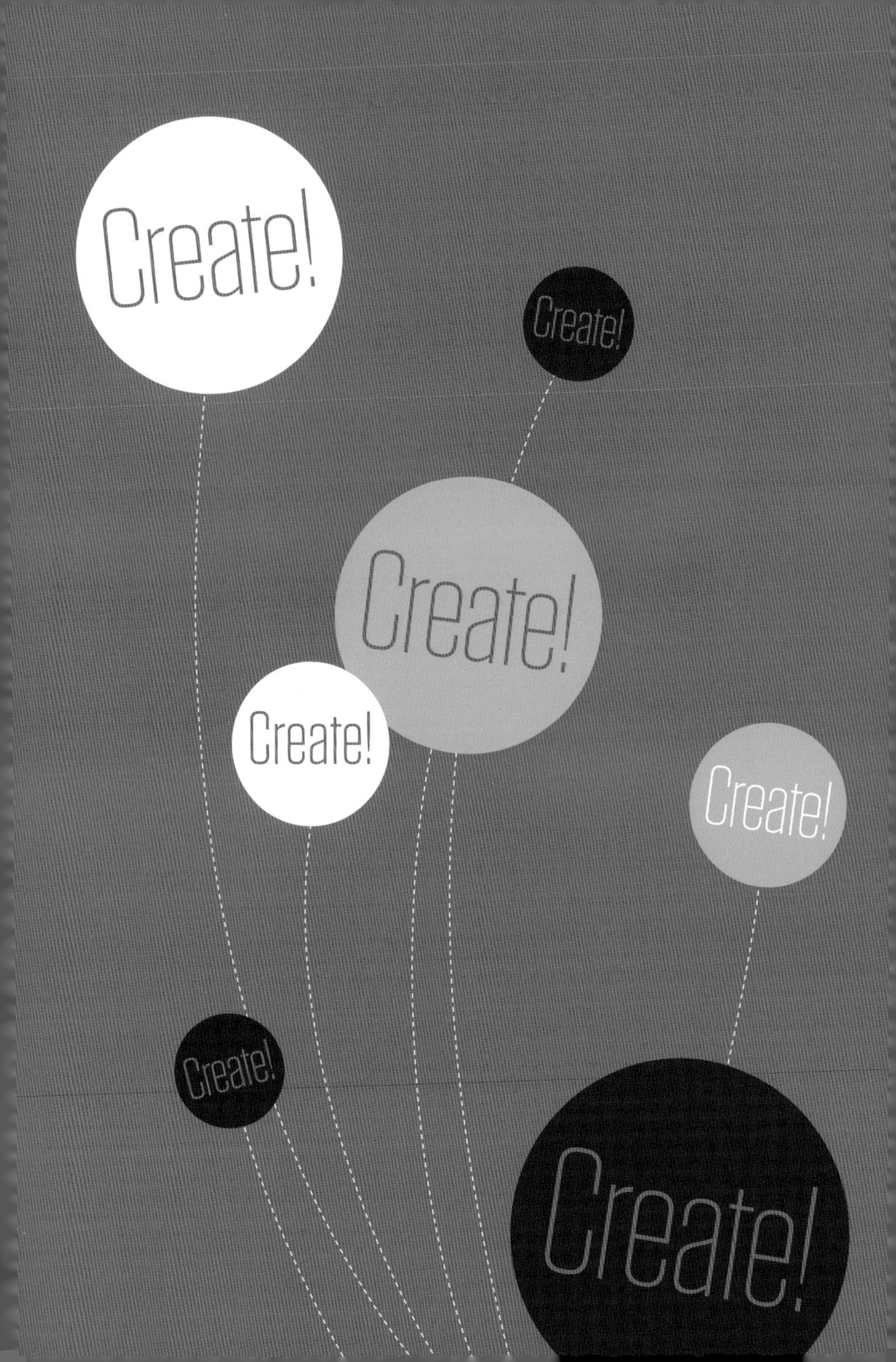
Create!
Create!
Create!
Create!
Create!
Create!
Create!

Instead of reacting,
I am CREATING.

Have you ever considered that the letters in "creation" and "reaction" are the same?

I have learned that when I am faced with any situation, I have a choice. I can either react to it or I can create in response to it.

When I reacted in the past, my response was usually based on fear. Or it was hasty or impulsive. Sometimes things worked out. Often I had regrets.

When I pause, consider, and think about what I can create, I can respond in many ways. I can see things from many angles and consider several options. I can invent ideas with imagination and pick from them. I can create the answer, the next action, and the course that will be right for me.

The opportunities we have to create are vast and far more dimensional than most people ever consider. The benefits of all kinds of creativity cannot be overstated.

When we create a drawing, a poem, or a gorgeously decorated cake; or play an instrument; or dance, we are creating in ways that open our hearts and connect us to our souls. And while many people find that trying that kind of creativity can feel daunting, when they do start making creativity a part of their lives, they experience new pathways of energetic flow, gain meaningful insights, and experience incredible joy.

In addition, what you may not think about when you consider the idea of creativity is that creativity can be employed all the time. In every moment, you can decide what you want to create in response to a situation or through your own initiative. You can slow down the impulse to habitually react and learn to create instead.

You can create, invent, and reinvent anything and everything. This sensitivity to creating is amazing, and it's something you can adopt easily when you become aware of how to use it and practice making it a regular part of daily life.

1 Start experiencing creativity—or ramp it up.

IN ADDITION TO MAKING "ART," which may feel intimidating, start by thinking about fun, simple ways of being creative. Try doodling with colors you love and sketching to make your ideas visual. Collect things that fascinate you, take photographs, cook more freely and creatively, sing in the shower—the possibilities are endless. Motivate yourself by going to galleries, concerts, or the circus. Take walks in nature. Visit any place that will stimulate and excite you to try your hand at creation.

2 Stimulate yourself by probing what excites you.

TO KICK-START YOUR THINKING and get yourself into action, try these Discovery Dozens:

"Something I'd really enjoy creating today is _____."
"It would be so much fun to experiment and try _____."
"If I knew nobody would judge me, I would create _____."

DISCOVERY 12 DOZEN

3 Use emotion as creative fuel.

A LITTLE-KNOWN BENEFIT OF CREATING is that doing so is a fabulous way to process emotion. When you use any emotion as fuel for a creative act, you bring passion to your efforts. Creativity is a perfect way to enhance positive emotions, as well as to process and transform difficult emotions. While it's easy to imagine how making a gorgeous drawing in bright colors would make your pleasure even richer, it may be harder to imagine using the act of creating to cope with tough feelings like anger, frustration, grief, pain, or fear. Once tried, it becomes easier to see that it's always safe to use raw emotions as creative fuel. In fact, doing so enables you to "download" those emotions and safely transform them.

There's a simple way to test this out. The next time you are feeling anxious or upset, pull out paper and colored markers or oil pastels. Deliberately make a hideously ugly picture—the ugliest one you can possibly make. While you are gouging the page with dark, mucky colors, focus on making your intense feelings visual. You might include words in your picture. Cover the entire page, edge to edge, with color. You may want to make more than one of these hideous pictures. Keep going until all the emotion is wrung out and on the pages. You will have unburdened yourself in a powerful way.

You may prefer to write a poem to express the big emotion, or process it through intense music, or by dancing it out. Any way you choose to create using emotion will work wonders.

4 Think about creating in each moment.

IN ADDITION TO EXPRESSING EMOTION through creative acts, consider every moment as an opportunity to create. You can create your next move in every situation. And, in doing so, you are creating the life you want.

Instead of reacting to what someone says or does, resist the impulse to respond to the situation as presented. Deliberately slow down and ask yourself what options you have, then decide what choice you want to make. Even when your options are not great, you get to make a choice. We have the power to create our next best decision at each point in time.

Keep in mind that you don't have to be "perfect" or make "perfect" decisions. Slow down, consider your options, make your best decision, course-correct as needed, and repeat.

5 Keep a journal.

A JOURNAL OR SKETCHBOOK is a wonderful tool to have on hand. It's a place for you to create on the spot—to record ideas, draw, paste in things that delight you—and it's also a place where you can keep notes about the ways you are creating in every facet of your life. You'll learn from it, inspire yourself, and feel empowered to expand the ways you bring creativity into your life.

6 Create with others.

INVITE A FRIEND OR ASK YOUR SPOUSE OR PARTNER to be your "creativity buddy." Or form a group to focus on creating together and sharing all the ways you come up with to use creativity in your lives. This will be motivating and will add to the pleasure of creating.

> **BIG IDEA**
> ## Cultivate Self-love, Manage Your Self-Critic
>
> *A strong foundation for living big and being a powerful creator is built on robust self-love coupled with learning to understand and keep your self-critic at bay.*
> *I've created a how-to guide to help you do both.*
>
> . . .
>
> **DOWNLOAD THE GUIDE AT**
> **TheLiveBigBook.com/gifts**

Speak Your
TRUTH

I found my truth
and speak it LOUD.

There is truth in all of us — it's authentic and personal.

Finding my truth required courage and trust—to look deep inside and to believe that I could go there and not be overwhelmed by pain. When I did, I was able to speak that truth out loud.

My opinions and truths were often not welcome as I grew up. I was trained to show up quietly, not rock any boats. Thus, it was hard to feel that my truth—when I connected to it—would be appreciated. It took time to find the courage to speak without second-guessing, without concern that I might displease people, and without fear of being ridiculed.

Finding my truth and having the courage to speak it were central to my personal growth. It changed my life and allows me to live big.

Few of us are fortunate enough to have been raised in a family and in school settings where we were encouraged to speak our thoughts and confidently voice our ideas.

It seems as if even fewer were taught how to connect to what their hearts desire, to shape independent thinking, and then share their insights and perspectives. For those who have been able to connect to the messages that reside in their hearts, few feel comfortable and confident about speaking their truth, be it with their families, in school settings, and, later, in their professional lives.

Fear is the primary force at play—fear of what we will find if we look inside, and fear of speaking our truths to the world. We fear that if we allow ourselves to be open, we'll be vulnerable. We may be criticized, and the prospect of the shame that will follow keeps us quiet.

Overcoming these limitations opens us to enormous growth. We are stronger, happier, and more inspiring to others when we connect to our truth and let it be heard.

1) Look into your heart.

THIS EXPLORATION MAY TAKE SOME TIME, so be patient with
yourself as you begin to mine your heart. Begin by doing Discovery
Dozens with these sentence roots.

"My biggest dream is _____."
"My heart wants me to know _____."
"If I dare to take a look into the depths of my heart, I will
find that _____."

DISCOVERY 12 DOZEN

Complete these sentences without fear. Let everything and anything
out onto your page—no one but you will see these sentences, and these
revealing messages are important.

If you find it difficult to do this exercise, try again on other days.
Or change the sentence roots as you wish to help you make the
discoveries you seek.

2) Discover what you really want.

THIS EXERCISE HAS TO BE DONE WITH A PARTNER. Invite
someone who is close to you, and whom you trust, to spend a few
minutes with you. You will both go on a journey of self-discovery.

Begin by sitting face-to-face. It may be across a small table or on
facing chairs with knees touching. You need to look deeply into one
another's eyes.

If you go first, the other person will be the "questioner." The questioner sets a timer for five minutes, and then asks, *"What do you want?"* You answer. The questioner immediately repeats, *"What do you want?"* You answer again. This continues on and on until the timer rings. If the questioner feels you are repeating yourself or not continuing to go deeper, they can say, "What else do you want?" After the timer buzzes, switch roles. You will set the timer and begin to ask, *"What do you want?"*

When the second round is complete, you will both have a lot to think about and discuss. People sometimes become quite emotional in this process, so be ready for that possibility. And be ready to surprise yourself with what comes up. Big insights can show up quickly, but more often it takes several minutes before deeper desires begin to emerge.

③ Now is the time to speak your truth.

MAYBE YOU'VE BEEN HOLDING BACK on things you've wanted to say for a long time. And maybe the new revelations that showed up in the first exercises are begging to be expressed.

In either case—or both cases—you may be nervous about speaking your thoughts, ideas, and needs, especially if you think that people will be surprised to hear these things from you.

Your self-critic may ramp up as you contemplate speaking up with your family, speaking your ideas in meetings, and standing up for what you want in your relationships. When your self-critic sends loud messages of doubt, fear, or warnings of impending ridicule, you need to step up your self-love to ward off those signals. This is the time to remind yourself of how amazing and smart you are and that you deserve to be heard. Treat yourself as the special person you are and tell your self-critic that for the next hour, you'll be so busy being awesome that you won't be listening to its warnings. As funny as that sounds, it really works to tell your self-critic to step aside for a while. That gives you a break from its damaging messages, and with self-loving reminders, you'll be able to test speaking your truth.

Begin by trying it in a safe place with people who will support you and encourage you. Start with expressing ideas that are new for them to hear, but not hugely dramatic. As you get comfortable, you can reveal bigger ideas. You can start to contribute more ideas at meetings, either at work or in family or community settings. The more you venture to speak up, the easier it will become.

Be prepared. Not everyone will agree with you all the time, and that's fine. Don't be defensive and try not to feel ashamed if people disagree with you. Own your ideas and your opinions. Ask for what you need and want. The more you practice speaking your truth, the more people will expect—and in many cases look forward to—hearing what you have to say.

The more you do this, the more you will find satisfaction in no longer holding yourself back or living small. Bravo!

BIG IDEA
Turn Desire into Action

Start with connecting to what you truly desire, and believe that you can create it. Begin—with commitment to taking small first steps, to playing and experimenting, to tapping your intuition as you go. Inspiration will fuel your efforts as you stay in action.

TAP YOUR
PASSION

My passion is my GUIDE.

When passion fuels my life, every day is exciting. It's easy for me to decide what to do—and what to say "no" to. It gives me focus, clarity, and energy.

My passion was always there, even though it had been hiding. I needed to break down the walls I'd constructed around my heart to connect to it. Learning to create was the tool that broke through the barriers and led me to my passion.

When I create as a regular part of my life—in every imaginable way, and in different ways on different days—I continually connect to my passion and confidently pursue it. I can write poems, paint, dance, sing, sketch, and cook with a creative spirit. Then I cannot help but feel my passion. I delight in it and trust it. My passion removes limits, and I live in a vast and thrilling world.

Legions of people struggle as they race on a daily treadmill. They feel drained and, often, burned out. Our culture celebrates that frantic pace, being ever-connected and super-productive.

People frequently tell me they can't find time for themselves—for the exercise they need and want, to eat well and with time to savor their meals, to pursue interests they long to explore, and more.

The irony is that people crave a connection to their passion and big meaning in their lives, but living at a non-stop pace makes it nearly impossible to do that. Stress and hurry are antithetical to the conditions that will allow them to tap their passions, or even pursue practices that will open access to those passions.

The good news is that it is possible to connect to your passion without a complete life overhaul. Small changes can a have huge impact, and, in time, more balance shows up too. Good things lead to more good things.

TRY THESE
EXERCISES
AND SEE
WHAT
HAPPENS
FOR YOU

① Create small pockets of time and use them well.

BABY STEPS CAN WORK WONDERS. Make a plan to take five-minute breaks at least twice a day this week. Think of them as mini-vacations! What will you do during these brief breathers? Just the pause will stop you from being in hyper-drive. Simply sit quietly in a spot away from the hubbub and breathe deeply. Take a short walk, or look at a beautiful view or the sky. Think about something for which you are grateful.

These breaks will refresh you. They'll give your energy a boost when you return to your tasks. And they will open channels to ideas and emotions that otherwise are crowded out.

② Add in some exploration.

NOW THAT YOU'VE TESTED these two-a-day short breaks, see what time of day you can add another five or ten minutes in—either as an extra break or as a longer break when you can pause.

Now, after you separate from your busy pace and shift into a more relaxed mode, you have a great opportunity to introduce some creative exploration. There are endless options for ways to be creative in small pieces of time. You might reflect on something that happened in your day and write a limerick to put a funny spin on it. Or doodle with brightly colored pens. Or go to a nearby shop and pick out a few crazy flowers, then take them back to your desk or kitchen and make a cool arrangement. Take a short walk and whistle some favorite tunes. Or dream up something to make for dinner that you never tried before and that you can do by improvising, instead of following a recipe.

③ Add more "you time" to create.

BY NOW YOU WILL HAVE REALIZED that the world did not implode when you made some small pockets of time for yourself. And you may have felt that the breaks provided a boost to your energy and enthusiasm when you got back to your usual tasks. Let's keep expanding that goodness!

Here are some easy, good ideas:

Rather than eating at your desk, make a commitment to taking time away to eat, either alone or with a friend who will provide stimulating conversation. Commit to devoting enough time to eat slowly, enjoy the food, and digest your meal.

Identify a particular way you like to create. It could be writing, singing, sketching, assembling found objects, gardening, cooking—really anything at all that brings you pleasure. Now set aside a little time in your calendar to pursue that creativity—perhaps during your daily breaks, and maybe by rearranging your schedule to open up a somewhat longer stretch of time.

Take a class focused on something you enjoy creating or want to try. Many places offer terrific adult ed classes. Arts and community centers have wide offerings. Start exploring options. You might pick a one-evening workshop at a local museum, or a series of evening or Saturday classes in a school or community center.

When you've made this kind of creativity a normal part of your life, you'll begin to feel new pleasure and satisfaction. The more you make creativity a habit, the more you will want to pursue it.

4 Connect to the passion that shows up.

MAYBE YOU ALWAYS WANTED TO SING but were told you didn't have the talent to make it—and now you're singing for fun all the time. Maybe you tried a sculpture class on a whim and discovered it's something you love that you had never even thought of doing before. Whatever creative outlet has engaged you will open doors in your heart. This is the time to continue creating and continue exploring creative avenues that intrigue you.

When you feel excited to start a creative project, or look forward to getting to class, or feel pride in something you created, you are connecting to excitement and passion. The desire you feel for learning a new craft or playing an instrument can be the gateway to big insights about almost anything—your relationships, the work you do, a future that you realize you want to work toward, or a volunteer endeavor that will bring you joy.

Whatever shows up may come as a big realization, or insights may seep into your consciousness gradually. Let it happen and be alert. When you feel that passion, rejoice in it, employ it, and continue creating to keep it alive and expanding.

5 Expand and accelerate the process.

CREATE IN AS MANY WAYS AS YOU CAN and you'll keep connecting to passion. You may be surprised by how much and in how many ways you can create, when finding time had once seemed impossible.

BO LIVE LDLY!

I must be bold to
LIVE BIG.

Being bold requires that I think big.
And it requires that I be big. I must speak and act
with energy that feels sure and clear and exciting.

I, like many others, did not live boldly for most of my
life. I didn't know how. I felt intimidated. And I felt
too vulnerable to even explore what being bold could
be—much less dare to try it out.

With support and loving encouragement, I discovered
and grew a beautiful boldness. It had existed inside
me all along. I just never saw that it was there,
yearning to be found.

Opening and growing into boldness has been one
of my life's greatest joys. It has had a huge, positive
impact—and it's here to stay.

When you think of living boldly, what do you think about? How does it feel to contemplate that way of showing up, making decisions, taking action, and speaking your mind? Can you imagine getting past the resistance, and the fear that may be sitting underneath it, to live boldly?

So much genius in our world is bottled up, never shared, and it never emerges to make the impact it is meant to—all because people hold themselves back. They resist the possibilities of thinking big and being bold. They curtail personal happiness.

Were you brought up to speak only when spoken to, to sit quietly and keep your thoughts to yourself? Or were you told you should settle for less than you sense might be possible? If so, it may feel intimidating to consider a shift to living boldly—or to even imagine how you might move in that direction. If you doubt that it's possible for you to live boldly, I urge you to experiment with it a bit here.

1 First, test your assumptions.

IT'S IMPORTANT TO IDENTIFY THE WAYS you are "programmed" to live without the level of boldness you want to explore and build. Start with this Discovery Dozen:

"It's hard to imagine living more boldly because _____ ."

When you look at your answers, you may want to explore deeper levels of insight. For instance, if one of your answer was something like, *"It's hard to imagine living more boldly because my grandmother always put me down when I tried to speak up for myself,"* you might follow up with another Discovery Dozen like, *"Even though I was put down then, I now realize _____ ."*

Or, for an answer like, *"It's hard to imagine living more boldly because it was safer to be seen and not heard,"* you might follow up with this Discovery Dozen: *"If I speak up a little more now, it will be different because _____ ."*

This type of digging for deeper insights will help you see the ways in which you adopted ideas that do not align with who you are now and what your possibilities are at this point in your life.

② How might you want to live more boldly?

ONCE AGAIN, THE DISCOVERY DOZEN is a great tool for identifying ways you can welcome more boldness into your life. Try these sentence roots:

"To live more boldly, I want to _____ ."
"It would be great to be more bold when _____ ."

These types of Discovery Dozen sentence roots will help you envision yourself growing bolder in ways you most desire. Whether your answers reveal that you yearn to courageously travel to remote places, make a big career change, or speak to a huge audience on the TED stage, the information you retrieve from this exercise will set some concrete visions and directions for you to move toward and will motivate you to take action.

③ Start to be bolder.

STARTING SOMETHING NEW is often a challenge. This is the time to bolster self-love and your belief in your talents and abilities—because you are amazing! Develop small rituals to remind yourself that you are unique and fantastic. You can put post-it notes where you'll see them at every turn (your alarm clock, bathroom mirror, coffee maker, etc.) with reminders about how wonderful you are and that the world is ready for you to be bolder.

In concert with bolstering self-love, pay attention to your desires to be bolder. When you really want something, you can cope with the fear that is likely to show up at first. So if you desire to venture out on a great excursion, or suggest a dynamic new idea at work, focus on why you want to do that and the great outcomes you can envision from taking those steps.

④ Small actions lead to boldness.

REMEMBER THAT BEING BOLD takes many forms. Make bolder decisions, rather than waffling. Focus on following through at moments when you feel doubt. Allow yourself to be a bit vulnerable and trust that people will see that as bravery they admire. Envision your ideas catching fire. Dare to go after opportunities. Show up in the clothes that showcase your true style.

No matter the responses you get, part of being bold is knowing that you are capable of rebounding if things do not always go perfectly.

⑤ Take stock and ramp it up.

WITH EACH NEW, BOLD ACTION YOU TAKE, reflect on the ways that you were courageous, the outcomes of the action, and the resilience you mustered. Acknowledge yourself for taking bold action! Then consider ways to accelerate the boldness—either in the same or in new directions.

⑥ Seek support and encouragement.

WE ALL NEED PEOPLE TO SUPPORT US, and when we are working to be bolder in our lives this is especially important. Think of people who will help you see big possibilities, champion your efforts, and encourage you when doubts arise or things have not gone perfectly. Ask them for the kind of feedback you want—to be brutally honest with you, or maybe to be gentle but firm. Ask them to help you to continue growing bolder over time, so you do not limit yourself. Keep looking for opportunities to live big and keep going for them. The sky is the limit!

[embrace
change]

I don't resist
CHANGE.

When change came suddenly in my never-static life, or was unexpected or unpleasant, fear and anxiety used to step right in.
And sometimes, good changes challenged me. They disrupted routines and norms that were comfortable. It felt unsettling to face a shift in the status quo.

Now I can calmly see a situation and respond without fear. I cope with change more easily.

I transform the stress of difficult emotions through creative acts—like writing, singing, or drawing the emotion onto a page. When I diffuse anxiety this way, I can see more clearly and find the ideas, decisions, perspectives, and answers I need. Then I move ahead, adjust, and get through the change. Often, I discover something unexpected—something wonderful I did not see coming.

Change is rarely easy. Individuals resist change, and groups and organizations are renowned for finding it challenging to work through.

We are wired to feel comfort with what is familiar, even when we are not satisfied with the status quo.

While there are change management experts out there to help with organizational change, how can we, as individuals, cope more easily with change in any part of our lives?

Happily, there are many ways you can learn to navigate and embrace change.

TRY THESE EXERCISES

➊ Look at what's going on.

START WITH IDENTIFYING THE CHANGE AT HAND. Are you being thrust into change by someone else? Do you need to initiate a change? In either case, you will feel some level of discomfort. Getting clarity on the situation is a good place to start.

The change can be internal or external, close to you or distant. This is a good time to thoughtfully consider the change and all of the dimensions that may be related to it.

Perhaps you are facing a move. Are you looking forward to the new home or new city, or do you feel forced to make the move? What upsides might there be, even if you are not eager for this move? What concerns are lurking, even if you are eagerly looking forward to it?

Perhaps your company is merging, and the new workplace structure is uncertain. There's surely going to be anxiety about how things will work out, but there may also be interesting opportunities.

Perhaps you are thinking about change in the political climate— change that excites you or feels worrisome. Or maybe you are contemplating a personal change that will entail big decisions and courage, even if the outcome is one you want to realize.

Whatever kind of change is in the air, start by taking a clear look at it and thinking about all the possibilities. There is usually a mix of positive and negative, so take stock by writing it all out. When you clearly see the upsides and downsides, you are less likely to be pulled by emotions that can interfere with your equilibrium.

② Actively assess so you can respond to your emotions.

AFTER YOU HAVE EVALUATED THE RANGE of your emotional responses, get down to the roots of your emotions—and their scope.

Do you feel anxious? Identify worst-case scenarios and also best-case possibilities. Are you excited? Consider what's joyful and test to see what ripples of concern may be under the surface.

Write about all of your feelings. Let them pour out quickly. Check in this way several times on different days. Next, write the key words and phrases that express your emotions. Look at what you wrote. Which emotions are drawn in letters that fill a page, and which words or phrases are so small you need to squint to see them? Visualizing the emotions this way will help you recognize those that hold the most and least energy related to your change. It will help you pay attention to all the emotions at play and identify which to reduce or boost to help you navigate the change.

③ Start creating with the emotions you have identified.

AS DESCRIBED IN EXERCISES #3 AND #4 in the "Create!" section (pages 73-74), use your emotions as fuel for creating in amazing ways—and create rather than react. This is the perfect time to process and transform difficult emotions by drawing ugly or angry pictures, dancing to loud music, pouring out a poem, or hacking away at vegetables when you cook. Create to elevate and encourage your positive emotions. Be inventive as you create with all of the emotions! Pay attention to what you want to create at every moment during this process, rather than being reactive as you go through this time of change.

Gain clarity and make decisions with good tools.

THIS IS AN EXCELLENT TIME to use a Discovery Dozen to resolve confusion and help you make decisions. Try some like these:

"When I think about this change, I feel _____."
"The tension I feel in my chest is telling me that _____."
"I can respond to the latest update from my boss by _____."

Trust yourself.

BY NOW, YOU HAVE TESTED NEW WAYS to identify and process your emotions, gain insights, and make good decisions. The creative tools available to you are vast and can be used for as long as you need them. Even when you are doing well, new surprises can crop up, so stay tuned to awareness of when and how you are feeling new emotional responses and keep using your tools.

A big key to navigating change is trusting yourself to pay attention and to take action to help you process, cope with change, and move forward, regardless of what comes at you along the way.

Celebrate!

HAVING NAVIGATED a period of change, you'll be on the other side of what once felt like a challenge. Acknowledge and celebrate every way you spared yourself anxiety or stress by using creativity to process your emotions and make good decisions. The precise outcome of change will vary in each situation, but your growing skills for coping with change are big steps to living big and are always worth celebrating.

Play
ENRICHES
and adds interest to my life.

Play is powerful. When I let myself play freely, I feel joyous and at ease, and my spirit opens.

While adults tend to stay alert, always making sense of the outer world, children at play are relaxed, yet focused, alert, lucid—and creative.

To get to that state, I close my eyes, soften my muscles, and relax as I take deep breaths. Then I easily begin to play. Fear drops away. I enjoy experimenting, and make discoveries that would not otherwise appear. Sure, mistakes sometimes happen, but I am not concerned about them. They are sometimes wonderful mistakes that bring me to new solutions and ideas and experiences. Or they can simply teach me something that will help me down the road. Play leads me to marvelous discoveries.

When was the last time you played freely? Lots of people feel that play has to be left behind when they reach adulthood.

Or they think their busy lives preclude play. When they have leisure time, they default to zoning out in front of a screen. They're sure they'd feel embarrassed or undignified at play.

The thing they likely do not understand or appreciate is that play, along with silliness and laughter, is incredibly healthy for humans of every age. Much as children learn through play, adults learn too. Play lets us stretch our imaginations and experiment freely. It fuels creativity and relieves stress. Our self-critical voice is sidelined as we play, and fear is quieted. We can rejoice in the delight and freedom of play, as well as all that we discover in the process.

1 Reconnect to the sensations of joyous play.

TO START PLAYING MORE, get back in touch with the delight of play. Go to a playground, beach, or party and watch kids play. Watch how inventive and fearless they are. Revel in that joy, focus, and ease. Take note of the creative ways they play—alone and with others. Think back to how it felt when you played as a kid. Then, think of at least three ways you can bring some of that energy into your life.

2 Consider your opportunities to play at work.

YOU CAN HAVE FUN simply dreaming up ways to play! Use this Discovery Dozen to generate ideas.

I can make things fun at work if _____ .

Your answers could include things like:

"I can make things fun at work if I put a basket of small toys on the conference room table so everyone can play for a few minutes before meetings."

"I can make things fun at work if I don't take everything so seriously."

"I can make things fun at work if I plan regular staff outings."

You might even ask your colleagues to use this Discovery Dozen. See what ideas show up for them, then choose at least one idea to start with, and add more—as often as possible!

And, if you generate an answer like this: *"I can make things fun at work if our meetings begin with everyone sharing a funny scene from a TV show they saw in the last week."* You can go deeper with another Discovery Dozen such as: *"A fun icebreaker to start meetings could be* _____ *."*

There are countless ways to bring more play into your work.

③ Use play when you struggle (at work or at home).

WHEN A GROUP AT WORK IS STRUGGLING to find a solution to a tough challenge, why not let play help break the logjam?

Let's say people are stuck, or feel intimidated to offer suggestions when new ideas are needed. Guide everyone to throw out a ridiculous idea. Make it a contest to see who has the most exaggerated suggestion. Set a rule that no idea can be shot down—they are all welcome! Do this for several rounds. Getting the group to laugh and loosen up enables fresh ideas to show up. Before long someone will build on an outrageous contribution, and start connecting dots in new ways. Fresh solutions are likely to emerge without stress.

A similar approach will work when a challenging solution is needed at home. Get ideas flowing freely with your spouse, kids, family members, or friends, and let awesome ideas emerge.

④ Consider ways to play more, and more often.

CONSIDER WITH WHOM you can create opportunities to play, like kids (your own or others'), pets, neighbors, your partner, or family members you rarely see. Use this Discovery Dozen to get started:

"To have more fun I/we can _____."

Your answers could include things like:

"To have more fun I can get the whole family to wash the car together and have a water fight."

"To have more fun we can share Sunday morning brunches with a neighbor and then play board games or play outdoors."

"To have more fun we can rotate choosing a crazy new ingredient to cook with every weekend."

Try variations like this, too:

"To have more fun when I travel/on vacation _____."

Your answers could include things like:

"To have more fun when I travel I can take the subway in Tokyo."

"To have more fun on vacation I can take the kids to a drive-in."

5 Create group experiences filled with play.

BE A CATALYST FOR MORE LAUGHTER AND FUN. Invite people to a gathering for the purpose of playing together. Dream up crazy ways to set the stage for play and silliness. (Why not make up a Discovery Dozen to generate ideas?)

Whether you choose outdoor activities, a cooking competition, a craft-centered activity, or a museum scavenger hunt, declare that seriousness is not welcome. Laughter, silliness and being open to all outcomes can be the explicit objective. Then gather and play!

And why not plan your next "play date" before you all say goodbye?

FIND

YOUR

WAY

CREATIVITY

resolves confusion.

Some days flow with clarity and purpose. Others are confounding. When my plans shift unexpectedly and time opens up, confusion can set in. I have an opportunity, but what to choose? How to pick from my long list of to-dos? This can be a nice dilemma, but it can nonetheless be unsettling. Or I may need to make a decision, but the choice is not clear. This used to provoke anxiety for me.

Now when I feel confused or unsure, I know I can create to find my way. I typically write or draw to tap and process the emotions I am feeling. I take a walk to release tension. I give myself space to let my intuition and imagination make rich connections to the "data" of my options. Then insights emerge that lead me to clear answers.

When there are pockets of time and no outside demands, or nobody's directing you, you are on your own to decide what to do.

This can leave you feeling confused, unsure, or anxious.

Or, if you are not already on task to complete a project, or don't have a clear trajectory in mind for a plan of action, you may be uncomfortable and unsure about what to do.

Or, something unexpected can appear, imposing challenges about what to do next.

Or, you may want to make a change, but it feels daunting to identify the right path.

You may feel out of alignment with coworkers and feel uneasy about how to proceed.

You may have a burning desire to make a big change, but choosing a direction is intimidating.

In any of these scenarios you can feel overwhelmed with options—or paralyzed with indecision.

But in any situation such as these there are always opportunities. We always have the choice of how to see our circumstances, and we can always choose ways to chart a course and move forward.

❶ Start by creating the space you need to get clear.

SIMPLY BEING QUIET AND BREATHING can help you open space and release the tension you may feel when you need to set a direction.

Sit where you can focus on your breath for two or three minutes. Inhale slowly to the count of four. Then hold that breath for four counts. Next, exhale to the count of four, and hold for four counts before your next inhalation. This "box breathing" technique gives your mind an assignment so that other thoughts and worries cannot rush in! More importantly, this technique calms your nervous system and centers you.

You might also take a walk, journal, listen to music, soak in a bath— choose whatever feels right to get yourself primed to find your way.

❷ Add meditation to your toolkit. Here's how.

PEOPLE WHO MEDITATE can tell you what research confirms: meditation offers tremendous benefits. But in the midst of a busy life, meditation can feel like one more thing on a long to-do list—a luxury you can't figure out how to make time for. You may feel uneasy because you don't know how to do it, or unsure about how to get started.

Here are some ways to begin and ease into an ongoing practice.

Try a meditation timing app.

There are a number of good apps to choose from. Spend a little time playing with the settings and features.

Start small.

Even a few quiet, calm breaths can be beneficial. In just a few minutes you can gain the benefits of slowing down and getting centered. Pick a time of day that works for you, set your app timer for two minutes, and simply sit and breathe. Don't try to quiet your mind. Just relax and feel your breath.

You don't need a totally quiet mind.

You might like listening to guided meditations. There are many good options; trial app subscriptions are a good way to check them out.

If you choose silent meditation and find thoughts coming into your mind, try one of these approaches. Listen for subtle ambient sounds. Focus on the feeling of your breath entering your body and the feeling of your exhales. Try using a word on your inhale, such as "peace," and a word for exhales, such as "release." Or, in pauses between your inhales and exhales, think "one" each time.

Slowly build time for meditation into your life.

Your two-minute meditation breaks will likely become such a refreshing pause that you'll want to start adding to the timer. Expand your sitting time gradually. Sit for four or five minutes, then add time until you sit for 10 minutes. It may take a few weeks before you are ready to add another two minutes. After a while, 15, 20, or 30 minutes may be the perfect amount of time for your meditation practice.

Congratulate yourself for committing to this practice.
Acknowledge yourself after your first week, each time you add a
minute or two, and when you have meditated for a full month. As
you feel the benefits, meditating can become a normal—and very
special—part of your life.

3 Now you'll be able to more easily generate options to explore.

WITH A CALM, QUIET MIND, encourage yourself to be open and
curious. The Discovery Dozen can help you generate ideas to consider.

Let's say you have a snow day that nixes your plans.
Suddenly you have unexpected time. A flood of thoughts
may come to you, or you may feel stumped and stuck. Try
one or more of these Discovery Dozens:

"Of the many possibilities I'm thinking of doing, _____
would be great to do today because _____ ."
"The most enjoyable way to spend part of my day would be to
_____ ."
"Something especially interesting I can do is _____ ."
"Something I have been putting off that would feel great to work on/
complete is _____ ."

For other scenarios, some of these Discovery Dozens may work well.

"The next step I can take to move my important project along
might be _____ ."
"A change I can make now to switch course could be _____ ."
"A change that could get me excited is_____ ."

You now have at least a dozen ideas. Star the one, two, or three that appeal to you the most. With this clarity about the choices that are best for you right now, you can start trying them out.

 ## Make a decision.

MAKING DECISIONS OFTEN BRINGS UP ANXIETY. Even with your selected ideas, you have to decide where to start.

This kind of anxiety is often rooted in the pressure of feeling that you must make the *right* decision—or a *perfect* decision.

Whether you are deciding what to do next, what solution to pursue, or which idea will work best, the pressure to choose a perfect answer is daunting. And it's counter-productive.

Simply look over your narrowed list of options and begin with the one that your intuition is most drawn to. You cannot make a bad decision here.

All of your options may be great, or they may all may fall short in some way. You will not know until you take action and see what happens. You can adjust if necessary! The ability to take imperfect action, and continue taking action at each step along the path, leads to amazing outcomes.

Make your decision now, and see what happens next.

 ## Reach out for support and encouragement.

WHEN YOU'RE FINDING YOUR WAY to longer-term change or are navigating tricky challenges, consider seeking out support.

Think of someone who truly cares about you and won't tell you what to do. Someone who can be a non-judgmental sounding board and who can help you expand your thinking is ideal. This may be an expert, a coach, or a wise person you know and trust.

Tell this person about what you're considering and the kind of help and encouragement you are looking for. Ask if they are interested and able to help you.

You may want to have a single conversation to get their feedback, or you may feel that a series of periodic meetings will be ideal. Make a plan and set it in motion.

6 Test, adjust, take more action, repeat.

ONCE YOU'VE STARTED TO TAKE STEPS—be it on a single day when you have unexpected open time or on a long-term path you've embarked on—you may find yourself feeling discouraged or unsure, or you may even get stuck.

What will help the most is your state of mind.

You can choose to adopt an attitude of willingness to test things. Stay open-minded and stay curious. Pause, reflect, and evaluate. Ask, "Is this working? Do I need to make adjustments, or is it time to switch to another option that I'd considered but not chosen to pursue?" Assess if you are being patient, or hastily rushing to judgment, or losing confidence. With an open mindset, you can continue making decisions and progress.

Keep moving one foot in front of the other, and you will find your way.

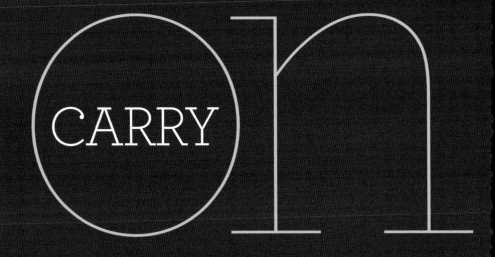

I can move through tough
CHALLENGES.

Life often seems fine until bumps appear in the road. When I rushed through my days, small bumps seemed normal, or best ignored. When bigger bumps came along—an emotional jolt, a health problem, a family issue, a surprising business setback—I used to get flummoxed.

I now avoid being blindsided. I move and live with more intention. I don't ignore minor issues. More challenging issues don't send me into a spin. I notice them readily and think about how and why they may have appeared. I quietly process my emotions. I consider how to cope with or resolve the matter. I find the path I need and know when I need to turn to trusted resources for help and guidance. I calmly use my head and my heart, and my inner compass guides me.

We all face issues that show up unexpectedly and can knock us off balance. Some things build slowly, and are especially challenging if we are not paying attention.

We often don't spot those early on, when they are easier to resolve. Other things can strike like a bolt of lightning and demand our attention and action. The ways we respond and are able to move forward profoundly color the experiences we have—and, in many cases, impact the outcomes.

When you are aware and pay attention, you can usually spot something coming. You can then think things out and plan your course of action before the challenge escalates. You may still find that you need to pivot and find a new solution or tactics, but you won't be caught off-guard. The practice of creatively thinking through multiple options can help you navigate your way.

And even when sudden, big challenges appear, if you develop skills for generating options and staying grounded—and practice them so they are readily available to you—you will be able to be resilient and carry on with more ease and grace.

1 ## Slow down and cultivate awareness.

YOU CAN LEARN TO PAY CLOSER ATTENTION TO—and pick up on—subtle as well as more obvious cues around you. But when you live in a state of overwhelm and overdrive, it's nearly impossible to do that.

What's required is to slow down. This means breaking the common habit of living in constant motion and with perpetual distraction.

You can start to consciously shift into a slower mode each day. Consider how you can build pauses into your day instead of scheduling back-to-back-to-back obligations. Consider what you can say "no" to, what you can delegate, and what you can defer.

Try some Discovery Dozens like these to generate ideas:

"I can do less of/stop _____ to live at a more sustainable pace."
"Something I can delegate is _____."
"I will be less distracted if I _____."

Next, look at your completed sentences and choose one or two ideas you can start using today.

Maybe you will commit to putting your phone away for longer periods of time, to be less distracted. Maybe you will put 20-minute "buffers" on your calendar between appointments so that you can reflect more.

Maybe you will step off of a committee that requires time and attention that tax your wellbeing.

Gradually add more changes until you are living at a pace that allows you more time to think and reflect. Then focus on turning your attention to reflecting.

Keep a journal on hand to note thoughts and insights while they're fresh. Color-code themes or topics so it will be easy to look back and connect the dots over time. Or, keep a file on your computer or device to capture moments of insight and observation. Note the date on your entries and tag them by topic. They will be easy to retrieve and review. Then be sure to schedule time to look back at your entries periodically.

You will feel a significant difference as you bring changes like these into your life, and you will notice that your awareness is keener.

2 Start taking early action.

SMALL CHALLENGES can often be nipped in the bud before they balloon into big problems. That's where your reflective notes can become valuable tools.

When you review your entries, be sure you are relaxed and not rushed. Many of your observations will be interesting, but not indicators of matters that need attention, so notice when your intuition pipes up and says, "Pay attention." Star those items, and take time to think about the message you are getting.

Maybe you will realize that a conversation is needed, or that facts need to be gathered or checked. Maybe you'll see how an obstacle might be turned into an opportunity. Creatively consider and list all the ways you can address the issues that have surfaced.

And, pay attention and catch yourself if you realize you've been in denial about a problem, or if you are worried about what to do and are tempted to push it aside. Connect to your emotions as you reflect. Stay alert and self-aware.

Then review your list of options and consider the three best ideas for taking action. From that short list you can choose the best step to start with.

③ Believe in yourself!

AS YOU START TO CONSIDER new ways to respond to challenges and think about doing things differently, you may feel hesitation. We are creatures of habit, and it's much more comfortable to respond in the ways we have in the past—or even avoid facing reality—than to devise and test new approaches.

You will likely find yourself needing to speak up, show up, or take action in ways that have not been your practice, and you may doubt your ability to do so.

This is a moment to sit and think about one or more times in the past when you have done something in spite of feeling doubtful. Give yourself evidence from your own life, and let that evidence build a belief that you can use to step into action and help you carry on.

The key is to act—even if it's not "perfect" action! Do your best and don't get discouraged. Persevere. This is how you build confidence.

Have tools on hand for when big stuff lands.

BIG SET-BACKS ARE INEVITABLE. There's an accident or illness or death, or a client loss impacts your career or business, or finances run short to address something urgent. While these sudden challenges are tough, they can be navigated more easily when you know how to approach them.

Begin by slowing down, getting quiet, and focusing on being present. Breathe—quietly and slowly! You may want to meditate. Emphasize self-care in as many ways as you can.

Realize that you are resourceful and you do have power—power you can harness to face the problem and move through it.

Rather than reacting, consider what you can create as your best next step, right now.

Consider people you can reach out to for support and guidance.

As you start to see your best next step to help you move forward, and the step after that, ask yourself questions like these below. Turn them into Discovery Dozens if you wish:

What is this here to teach me?
What would I do if I were not afraid?
How is this situation calling me to grow, expand, or adapt?
What am I learning now?

Share and celebrate each small victory as you find your way.

5. Learn from your experiences.

AS YOU DEVELOP SKILLS OF AWARENESS and a practice for checking in and taking early action to address challenges—or when you are faced with bigger challenges—you will have a terrific new opportunity. You will now be able to reflect on what has worked, and what has not worked, and use these insights to your advantage.

As you take new kinds of action and become comfortable with those responses, you will have experience to call on when similar challenges come up again, whether they show up unexpectedly or are spotted early on.

6. Appreciate and acknowledge yourself.

WHEN YOU FULLY APPRECIATE YOURSELF for your willingness and ability to learn and grow as you build important skills for carrying on, you will more easily be able to bring additional positive change into your life. This kind of acknowledgment helps bolster your growing confidence and builds self-love. You are also able to bring more boldness to facing whatever comes your way.

MOVE
INTO
THE

FUTURE

I boldly venture
FORWARD.

Even when I am not sure precisely where I am headed, I know there is more waiting for me. I stay alert to doors that may appear and, if my intuition tells me to open them, I try something new. My true path was waiting on the other side of those doors in the past.

So I test new opportunities to see if they are heart-poundingly exciting.

I do not fear the journey. I trust that my road will take me to a great destination. I connect to myself at a deep level and believe that enlightening discoveries await me.

I listen to my heart. It is a brilliant guide. I trust my intuition. I activate creativity in new and exciting ways. My creativity always powers a beautiful and remarkable process.

Most adults feel that life is what it is, as it is—whatever their career and work situation may be, whatever the quality of their relationships, whatever their role in the family and/or the community.

Some are complacent, some are resigned, some are afraid. They choose to continue living as things are.

But even those who desire change in their lives may feel stuck. They may want something new, sense that more is possible, or desire something different, and yet are unsure of what that may be, how to explore it, or how to take steps toward a more joyful future.

Because you are reading this book, you are likely to be a person who does not want to live a static life.

Whether you are living a satisfying, full life or you are frustrated or dissatisfied in some way, you want to grow. You want to live a fully creative life that evolves and expands. There is always space for more happiness, more challenge, more growth and insight, and more possibility.

That's the kind of life you can experience every day, the kind of future you can continually move into. You can choose to live big, and you can do it.

1 Always be guided by your desire.

WHEN YOU WAKE EACH DAY, ask yourself a series of questions:

- ▶ What do I want?
- ▶ What will bring me happiness, or enhance the happiness I feel in the moment?
- ▶ What does my heart yearn for right now?
- ▶ What is my gut trying to tell me?
- ▶ How can I make today amazing?

Any time you hit a moment of indecision or confusion, ask yourself these questions again.

Smile as you think about what you want and what you can create.

Your ideas may impact your next five minutes in an amazing way. Other answers may start you on a path of change that will entail many decision points and steps, and will make your life look remarkably different a year or five years from now.

2 Start creating your future in small but powerful ways.

AS YOU CONTINUE TO ASK QUESTIONS and hear answers, focus most on the ideas that are speaking the loudest and showing up the most often. They matter most.

BIG IDEA

Continually Create Your Future

I created the Roadmap to Clarity *to help you any time you are pondering questions and want to bring real change into your life.*

. . .

PURCHASE
this powerful tool, that can be used over and over.
TheLiveBigBook.com/clarity

And don't dismiss small things. For instance, if you notice a desire to listen to a genre of music that connects to your heart (whether it's opera, bluegrass, sentimental standards, or rock), start a practice of listening to that music on your commute rather than tuning into news updates. Or, make that music your morning soundtrack. Or, follow your mood and choose different music each time. But make music a part of your life.

If you've always enjoyed writing but have stopped as you focused on your family or career, why not commit to writing just five minutes a day? Then gradually schedule in more time as you enjoy the satisfaction of returning to something so meaningful.

If you've settled for take-out and eating out most of the time and miss cooking, schedule time to cook at least one new dish a week. As you enjoy seasoning, stirring, and presenting a beautiful meal, you'll connect to pleasure that you've been missing. You'll want to do this more often.

If you've always wanted to try a new sport or activity, start now. Sign up for tennis lessons, or join a group that hikes on weekends, or see if Zumba classes are offered at the local Y, or join a community chorus.

Even small changes such as these will open your heart and fuel your spirit. The creativity and energy will encourage you to make changes in other parts of your life. You are "priming the pump" for more joy and expansion.

126   Live Big

③ Take small steps toward making bigger changes.

WHEN YOU GET THE MESSAGE that a major shift is in order—such as a change in your closest relationship, pursuing an advanced degree, following an urge to do the work your heart was set on before you were steered to something more "practical," or making a move to a faraway place you've always dreamed of living—you are likely to feel nervous and doubtful about what's possible or what this change will entail.

It's normal to feel overwhelmed at the prospect of making a major life change. But that does not need to limit you.

When you want something important, and you believe that you are a creator, you know that creation is always possible!

The way forward is to generate ideas for getting started on your path, and to start taking steps in that direction.

You may begin by doing research or seeking advice or help. You may embark on experimenting with possibilities. Your first step may be mapping out scenarios or paths.

From there you will be ready to assess and create your next step.

Each small step you take—and your ongoing commitment to continue creating and taking next steps—will lead you to the future you deeply desire.

④ Stay positive and focused.

THINK ABOUT THE WAYS you can move into your ideal future smoothly and easily. You have a lot of opportunity to create an environment that will support you to live big.

Consider spending time with people who will lovingly support you and champion what you set out to do. Share your ideas, questions, and progress with them. Celebrate milestones with them, too.

Consciously create distance from people who will cast doubt, be negative, or try to dissuade you from creating the life you want. (Avoid those who feel jealous, or insecure seeing you grow and making bold strides, or will worry excessively, or tend to be negative for any number of reasons.) You needn't be harsh as you shift away from spending time with those who, even if they mean well, will dim your confidence or question your objectives.

To stay focused, track ideas and progress in a journal, or use a white board or a wall of post-it notes, or create spreadsheets. You may want to ask someone to be an accountability partner and have regular check-ins. You may seek out a coach to guide and support you on your journey. Or, you may find that a combination of these approaches will keep you moving forward to the future you want.

5 **Continually connect to what you truly want.**

WHENEVER YOU NEED TO STEP BACK and get some validation or fresh perspective, you can return to the exercise I shared on page 79 that guides you to sit with a partner and ask, again and again, "What do you want?" It's a powerful way to check in with your heart and connect to your deepest desires.

Because you have many desires, and there are many ways you can live a big life. There's no limit to what is possible.

Even as you may be focused on making a big change in your life, many small important changes are possible at the same time. Asking, "What do I want?" on different days will bring different desires to light.

You can always create in new and amazing ways.

Today you may want to bring more love into your life, or live more boldly, or cultivate patience. You may have a desire to play more, or to create with color in a way you've never tried before. You may realize you need to speak your truth to someone, or that it's time to slow down and be fully present, to find your way.

Use this book as a resource, and let it be a springboard to a magnificent future.

THIS IS **YOUR TIME.**

LIVE BIG!

Each of us can write our own
manifesto for creating the
life we want, populating it with
the ways we want to live big.

I invite you to dive in and
create your manifesto.
And I hope you will choose—
each day—to live big as you
define it for yourself.

With love,

Rochelle

Acknowledgments

THE JOURNEY OF MY LIFE would not have been the same without the abundant and exquisite love of my dearest husband, Steven. He has always believed in me and always seen more greatness in me than anyone else.

My children, Daniel and Gabriel, are my most magnificent creations. They inspire me endlessly, and their love fuels my heart every day.

Enormous thanks to my teacher, Dr. Pinki Feinstein, who opened my eyes and my heart to the power and accessibility of creativity and whose teaching and encouragement made my work possible.

My deep gratitude to my dear friend, coach, and mentor, Peleg Top, whose ongoing support and love have been invaluable, and for offering to write the foreword for the book.

The design of this book invites the reader to engage joyfully with the content. Mary Lester brilliantly brought the book to life with color, patterns, and exquisite typography that surpassed what I had envisioned—and I always saw this as a beautiful book in my mind's eye! I am grateful for both her talent and friendship.

My editor, Maggie McReynolds, brought a keen eye to the manuscript and supported me as we moved through the final stages of this project.

Last, I thank my remarkable clients, who have trusted me to guide them and who have taught me so much. Their courage and willingness to engage fully in our work has been beautiful to witness.

About the Author

ROCHELLE SELTZER BEGAN HER CAREER as a designer and led her firm, Seltzer, for 27 years. After selling her business in 2011, she embarked on a new chapter in her life, intensively studying creativity and developing a personal creative practice for the first time.

Rochelle's Creative Core Coaching practice embeds creativity into every client engagement. She supports accomplished women in overcoming limitations by accessing and accelerating their innate creativity and teaches them to use creativity in myriad ways to live their biggest lives.

In addition, helping individuals and corporate teams to understand, embrace, and leverage creativity to live big, work big, love big, and thrive is a key theme in her signature workshops, programs, and talks.

Rochelle lives in Brookline, Massachusetts, and works with clients locally, across the United States, and internationally.

In addition to her work as a master coach, Rochelle began to devote time to being an artist in 2015. Her paintings and drawings have been included in juried exhibitions and shown in galleries.

Rochelle's dream is for people everywhere to understand, trust, and use the power of creativity in their lives so that everyone can live big.

To explore Rochelle's Creative Core Coaching, visit
RochelleSeltzer.com.

To see Rochelle's artwork, visit
RochelleSeltzerArtist.com.

YOUR GO FORWARD PLAN

① Download Your Gifts

I HOPE YOU NOTICED THAT THERE ARE GIFTS from me to you sprinkled throughout the book. I want you to get the most out of *Live Big*, so be sure to grab your gifts:

- **Live in the Present** Guided Meditation
- **Find Patience** Guided Meditation
- **Self-Love and the Self-Critic** How-To Guide
- **Finding Your Way** Guided Meditation

DOWNLOAD THEM TODAY AT **TheLiveBigBook.com/gifts**

And, you can purchase my powerful **Roadmap to Clarity**. I'm offering it at a very special price for readers of *Live Big*. GO TO **TheLiveBigBook.com/clarity**

② Get the "Live Big Workbook"

LIFE IS BETTER WHEN WE COLLABORATE! In this companion guide to *Live Big*, you'll have tools and structure to help you dive in and do the work. Gather up a buddy, a few friends, or share it with your book club, and create your Live Big life together.

PURCHASE IT AT **TheLiveBigBook.com/workbook**

③ Leave a Review, Share the Process

IF THIS BOOK HAS IMPACTED YOU AND INSPIRED YOU, please go to Amazon.com and leave a review so that future readers can know how *Live Big* is already changing your life. And while you're on Amazon, be sure to buy a copy of *Live Big* for your friend, colleague, school, or library!